PUPPET SKITS

D1706414

David C Cook
transforming lives together

Cool Puppet Skits for the Park Patrol to Perform

NOAH'S PARK® CHILDREN'S CHURCH PUPPET SKITS (Red Edition)
Published by David C. Cook
4050 Lee Vance View
Colorado Springs, CO 80918 U.S.A.

David C. Cook Distribution Canada
55 Woodslee Avenue Paris, Ontario, Canada N3L 3E5

David C. Cook U.K., Kingsway Communications
Eastbourne, East Sussex BN23 6NT, England

David C. Cook and the graphic circle C logo are registered trademarks of Cook
Communications Ministries.

Editor: Carol Pitts
Contributing Writer: Sheila Seifert
Interior Design: Mike Riester
Cover Design: Todd Mock
Illustrations: Aline Heiser, Chris Sharp

All Scripture quotations, unless otherwise stated, are from the Holy Bible, New
International Version®, NIV®. Copyright © 1973, 1978, 1984 by Biblica,
Inc.™ Used by permission of Zondervan. All rights reserved worldwide.
www.zondervan.com

ISBN 978-0-7814-4493-4

First Printing 2007
Printed in the United States

5 6 7 8 9 10 11 12 13 14

032912

TABLE OF CONTENTS

INTRODUCTION

Puppets can be a great addition to a children's ministry program. Through the use of puppets Bible truths can be reinforced and the children can gain a better understanding of how to apply these Bible truths to their own lives.

Two puppets are included in this Children's Church Kit. The puppet personalities are listed on RP·5 of this book. After you identify your puppets and understand their personalities, it can help as you or the Park Patrol members present the puppet skits. (If you would like to purchase additional puppets to use in your program, call 1-800-323-7543 or visit our website at www.davidccook.com.)

There is one puppet skit provided to correlate with each week's Bible story. For the puppet skit presentation, we suggest that you combine the Elementary and Preschool children. If you have an exceptionally large Children's Church and would like to keep the Elementary and Preschoolers separated for the entire program, you might want to consider having more than one puppet theater and purchasing additional puppets.

You will want to train the Park Patrol members by using the Park Patrol Training Book. This training will help them confidently use the puppets and present the skits.

Have fun as you use these puppets and skits. Remember that this is a ministry that can have a great impact on your students!

PERSONALITIES

PONDER the Frog

Ponder the frog is the leader that everyone looks up to in Noah's Park. He watched Noah and Noah's relationship with God and now tries to help the other animals understand how God can help them in their everyday lives. Favorite quote: "I remember the ark!"

HONK the Camel

Honk the purple camel hates dirt; he loves to be clean. Honk is proud of his looks, from his clean and shiny fur to the proud gleam in his eye. Favorite quote: "I'm one good-looking camel."

DREAMER the Rhinoceros

Dreamer the blue rhinoceros is a very sweet and very sleepy animal. Dreamer loves to sleep, loves to dream, and loves to dream about sleeping. Favorite quote: "When I dream, I can do anything!"

STRETCH the Giraffe

Stretch the giraffe is the big sister to all the animals in Noah's Park. She is kind, generous, and very naive. Favorite quote: "I am curious about everything!"

HONK

STRETCH

DREAMER

PONDER

PUPPET THEATERS

Set up your puppet theater in a place apart from the Bible story area or the snacks, games, and crafts areas. That way the Park Patrol members can be setting up and be prepared to perform the day's puppet skit just as soon as you move the children to the puppet skit location. It will also make it obvious to the children that this is a special part of the program.

The following suggestions are given for some simple puppet theaters. Decide on the type of puppet theater by considering the space you have available and the cost of preparation. Be sure to have the puppet theater constructed before working with the Park Patrol for training. They will need to actually use the puppet theater, puppets, and skits as they practice to become proficient for this part of your program.

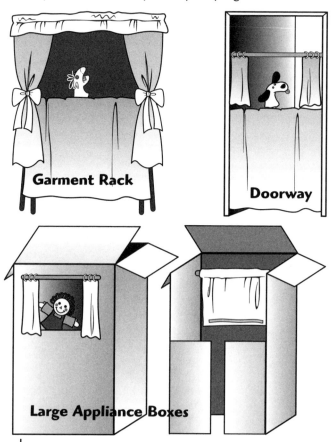

Garment Rack

Doorway

Large Appliance Boxes

RP1: Shooting Stars

Cast: Ponder the Frog, Noah's Park Puppet 2

Ponder is onstage looking at the night sky.

PONDER: *What a beautiful night.*

PUPPET 2:   (*Enters at a run.*) *Run for your lives!*

PONDER: *What's the matter,* (name of Puppet 2)*?*

PUPPET 2:   *Get out of the way! The sky is shooting stars!*

PONDER: *Shooting stars?*

PUPPET 2:   *That's what my mother said. I'm trying to warn everyone to take cover before it's too late!* (*Runs around the stage yelling, "Shooting stars!"*)

PONDER: *Hold on,* (name of Puppet 2)*. There's nothing to worry about.*

PUPPET 2:   *Maybe not for you, but there are a lot of animals who have nowhere to hide and might be hit by the shooting stars. They have to be warned!*

PONDER: *Did you ask your mother what she meant by shooting stars?*

PUPPET 2:   *No.*

PONDER: *Then stop and listen.* (*Puppet 2 stops running.*) *Look up at the night sky.*

PUPPET 2:   *Is it safe?*

PONDER: *Of course it's safe. God created the heavens, moon, and stars. His creation can be trusted.*

PUPPET 2:   *Okay.* (*Looks up.*) *What am I looking for?*

PONDER: *There. See that star?*

PUPPET 2: *Yeah. Wait. It made a line of light and then disappeared.*

PONDER: *That's a shooting star.*

PUPPET 2: *That's a shooting star? (Ponder nods.) That looks far away.*

PONDER: *It is, millions of light years away. Your mother probably meant that if you look into the sky tonight, you'll see a lot of shooting stars. She would have warned you if there was any danger.*

PUPPET 2: *Whew! Boy, am I relieved.*

PONDER: *Look, there's another one.*

PUPPET 2: *That is cool. Hey, did you say that God's plan for creation could be trusted?*

PONDER: *Yes, I did.*

PUPPET 2: *Then I suppose that day and night are safe.*

PONDER: *Yes, God made the earth, day, night, and sun.*

PUPPET 2: *Good. I heard that it might be daylight savings time soon, and I wasn't sure how to do it.*

PONDER: *Do what?*

PUPPET 2: *Save the daylight. (Yawns.) Well, if no one's going to get shot by stars tonight, I'm going home. Trying to save the world is tiring.*

PONDER: *Good night, (name of Puppet 2). Pleasant dreams.*

PUPPET 2: *They'll be pleasant now that I know I can trust God's plan in creation—and my mom.*

(Exit.)

RP2: Beautiful and Useful

Cast: Ponder the Frog, Noah's Park Puppet 2

Ponder and Puppet 2 face each other as if in the middle of a conversation.

PUPPET 2: *It's beautiful.*

PONDER: *And useful.*

PUPPET 2: *No, beautiful.*

PONDER: *But also useful.*

PUPPET 2: *Ponder, look at the ground. Have you ever seen such a great color of brown? It's beautiful!*

PONDER: *That is a nice color, but we also walk on the ground, and plants grow out of the ground. That's where they get their food. It's beautiful AND useful.*

PUPPET 2: *Okay, maybe the ground is useful. That was a bad example. Look at that plant over there. (Points to the audience.) It's a fern with lacy leaves. Have you ever seen something so small and beautiful?*

PONDER: *You're right.*

PUPPET 2: *I knew it. It can't be eaten. It's just beautiful, not useful.*

PONDER: *But that plant also breathes in carbon dioxide and breathes out oxygen. We breathe in that oxygen. All plants are useful.*

PUPPET 2: *Oh. I didn't know that.*

PONDER: *Plants are beautiful AND useful.*

PUPPET 2: *Another bad example. Wait a minute. (Looks up.) How about clouds?*

PONDER: *They are beautiful.*

PUPPET 2: *Right. They're light and fluffy. Hey, that one looks like you!*

PONDER: *Definitely beautiful, but I'm afraid they're also useful. They give us shade, and rain comes from the clouds.*

PUPPET 2: *Beautiful and useful. Well what about the rain itself? Water is . . . oh, wait, I know that one. It's beautiful, but we need it to drink. It's useful, too.*

PONDER: *The world that God created for us is beautiful AND useful.*

PUPPET 2: *I agree. I just wish I were right, too.*

(Ponder laughs. Both exit.)

RP3: Animal Sounds

Cast: Ponder the Frog, Noah's Park Puppet 2

Props: Background sounds of different animals in this order: frog, lion, frog again, bird, frog, elephant, frog, and then many frogs at once.

Ponder and Puppet 2 are listening carefully to the animal sounds around them.

PUPPET 2: *Okay, it's my turn to guess. (Both puppets listen carefully. "R-r-r-r-ibbit" is heard in the background.) It's a beaver.*

PONDER: *No, that was a frog.*

PUPPET 2: *Your turn.*

PONDER: *Okay. (Both puppets listen. A lion's growl is heard.) A lion.*

PUPPET 2: *Good one. My turn. (Both puppets listen. "R-r-r-r-ibbit" is heard.) A horse.*

PONDER: *No, that was a frog.*

PUPPET 2: *I always miss that one. Your turn.*

PONDER: *(He nods, and they listen. A bird whistles.) A bird.*

PUPPET 2: *That is sure a pretty sound. My turn. (They listen. "R-r-r-r-ibbit" is heard.) A wolf.*

PONDER: *That was a frog, again. (They listen. An elephant is heard.) An elephant.*

PUPPET 2: *You're good at this. (They listen. "R-r-r-r-ibbit" is heard.) A raccoon?*

PONDER: *No, still a frog.*

PUPPET 2: *God made so many creatures—fish, birds, mammals, reptiles, and insects. Why do I keep getting frogs?*

PONDER: *We are in a frog pond.*

PUPPET 2: *Okay, I'm going to get the next one.* (They listen. There is the sound of many frogs.) *That's a hard one.*

PONDER: *Kids, don't let* (name of Puppet 2) *make a mistake. What did he just hear?* (Let children shout the answer.)

PUPPET 2: *Are you sure, kids?* (Let the children answer.) *Then there's only one thing that that sound could be.*

PONDER: *That's right. Just say it.*

PUPPET 2: *I think it's a bunch of flies fighting over the water at the pond.*

PONDER: (Groans.) *God made so many animals, but He only made one that says, "Ribbit." Kids, tell* (name of Puppet 2) *what animal says, "Ribbit."* (Let the children say, "Frogs.") *Thank you.*

PUPPET 2: (To kids.) *Wow. God created so many kinds of animals, but you really know your animals.* (To Ponder.) *Let's let the kids play with us the next time we play this game, Ponder.*

PONDER: *That's a great idea, and next time, let's not play so near the frog pond.*

(Exit.)

RP4: Pond Pushers

Cast: Ponder the Frog, Noah's Park Puppet 2

Puppet 2 is pacing back and forth. Ponder enters.

PONDER: *What are you doing?*

PUPPET 2: *I'm protesting.*

PONDER: *About what?*

PUPPET 2: *I want to be in charge sometimes.*

PONDER: *In charge of what?*

PUPPET 2: *Everything.*

PONDER: *You want to be like God?*

PUPPET 2: *No, not God, like Noah.*

PONDER: *Oh, you want to be in charge of all the animals and take care of the earth.*

PUPPET 2: *Yeah. It's unfair that Noah gets to be in charge all of the time. He's just another animal like us.*

PONDER: *No, he's not. Noah is a person.*

PUPPET 2: *I knew you were going to bring that up.*

PONDER: *Maybe you don't understand.*

PUPPET 2: *I do, but some animals were created on the fifth day, and others were created before people on the sixth day. People were created last. That means that animals came first. We should be in charge.*

PONDER: *That makes sense, except that God put Adam and Eve in charge of everything He created. If you want to protest your place on earth, you'd better take it up with God.*

PUPPET 2: *I don't want to argue with Him. He's always right. I don't like losing.*

PONDER: *God also made people in His likeness. He didn't make us animals to be like Him.*

PUPPET 2: *I still want to be in charge.*

PONDER: *What do you want to be in charge of?*

PUPPET 2: *I want to be in charge because I'm tired of being pushed into the pond whenever I get a drink of water.*

PONDER: *So, you don't really want to run everything.*

PUPPET 2: *No, not really.*

PONDER: *What if I told your prankster friends to stop pushing you in the pond?*

PUPPET 2: *Would you?*

PONDER: *If you'll stop protesting and let Noah do what God has told people to do, I'll tell them.*

PUPPET 2: *Okay. Can you tell them right now? I'm really thirsty.*

PONDER: *Let's go.*

(Exit.)

RP5: Following Signs

Cast: Ponder the Frog, Noah's Park Puppet 2

A sign with a large arrow on it and the word "Detour" is onstage.

Puppet 2 enters. Ponder enters behind Puppet 2.

PUPPET 2: *What a mess.*

PONDER: *What's the matter,* (name of Puppet 2)*?*

PUPPET 2: *Didn't you see what happened?*

PONDER: *To the pond?*

PUPPET 2: *Of course, to the pond. It's rained so much that the pond has flooded. Now I have to get to my friend's house, and I don't know how to get there.*

PONDER: *There's only one thing to do.*

PUPPET 2: *I don't want to swim.*

PONDER: *Not swimming. Follow the arrows. Noah put them up so we'd know how to get around the pond. He has a lot of experience with floodwaters.*

PUPPET 2: *Is that what that sign is for?* (Points to the sign.)

PONDER: *Yes, it points in the direction that you should go to get around the pond.*

PUPPET 2: *I don't know if this is going to work. I need to go that way* (points in opposite direction of arrow)*, and the arrow says to go that way* (points in direction of arrow)*.*

PONDER: *I understand your confusion. Adam and Eve thought the same way that you did.*

PUPPET 2: *They were here?*

PONDER: *No, I mean a long time ago in the garden. God told them to do one thing, but they did what they thought was best.*

PUPPET 2: *What happened?*

PONDER: *God had to correct them.*

PUPPET 2: *That doesn't sound good.*

PONDER: *It wasn't. If you don't follow God's signs, you'll do what's wrong, and there are consequences.*

PUPPET 2: *I thought you said that this was Noah's sign.*

PONDER: *It is, but Noah is telling us what to do, because he cares for us. So if you don't do what his signs tell you to do, there are going to be consequences, too.*

PUPPET 2: *Like what?*

PONDER: *Like you'll end up in the water or mud or something else.*

PUPPET 2: *I've already done that twice. Maybe you're right. This time, I'll follow the signs.*

(Exit.)

RP6: God Saves

Cast: Ponder the Frog, Noah's Park Puppet 2, Mother of Puppet 2 (voice offstage)

Ponder and Puppet 2 are onstage.

PUPPET 2: *Tell it one more time, pleeeeease.*

PONDER: *I've told you Noah's story seven times.*

PUPPET 2: *I know, but it's so good. I like the part where God saves Noah and his family.*

PONDER: *Noah was a man who obeyed God.*

PUPPET 2: *Or maybe tell me about the rainbow. I like that part even better.*

PONDER: *Are you sure that's the part you want to hear about?*

PUPPET 2: *Oh, yeah. You can tell me how the rainbow is a symbol of God's promise not to flood the whole earth ever again.*

PONDER: *I don't think I will.*

PUPPET 2: *Why not?*

PONDER: *You just told me that part.*

PUPPET 2: *But I didn't say it like you do.*

PONDER: *Why do you like Noah's story so much?*

PUPPET 2: *Because it shows how God can save us no matter how bad the problem looks.*

PONDER: *True.*

PUPPET 2: *Even if we're stuck in a mud hole.*

PONDER: *God can save us.*

PUPPET 2: *Even if we can't swim, and we're in a river full of rapids and an alligator is chasing us.*

PONDER: *God can save us.*

PUPPET 2: *Even if we're at the top of the tree in the middle of a tornado and we're late for dinner.*

PONDER: *God can save us.*

PUPPET 2: *Even if we've lost our way, and don't know—*

MOTHER OF PUPPET 2: *(Offstage.)* **Time to eat,** *(Puppet 2)***!**

PUPPET 2: *That's my mother. I'd better go. Bye, Ponder. Thanks for all the stories.*

PONDER: **Bye.** *(Ponder waits until Puppet 2 is gone. He turns to the kids.)* **And God can even save us from having to tell the story of Noah's adventures for the eighth time in a row today. Say it with me, kids, "God can save us."** *(Repeats it with the kids. Exit.)*

RP7: Pond Jumping

Cast: Ponder the Frog, Noah's Park Puppet 2

Ponder is onstage. Puppet #2 hurries out.

PUPPET 2: *Ponder, will you jump over the pond later today?*

PONDER: *Okay.*

PUPPET 2: *I'm going to bring my whole family to watch how high you can jump.*

PONDER: *Okay.*

PUPPET 2: *You promise to be there?*

PONDER: *Yes.*

PUPPET 2: *Then we'd better do the Promise-Promise-Yes-I-Promise-Pact.*

PONDER: *The what?*

PUPPET 2: *Promise-Promise-Yes-I-Promise-Pact.*

PONDER: *What's that?*

PUPPET 2: *If you really promise that you'll be there, then hold up your hand.* (Ponder and Puppet 2 hold up their hands.) *Now jump three times.* (Both puppets jump three times.) *Then say, "Blpblpblpblpblp."* (Only Puppet 2 says it.) *You've got to say it.*

PONDER: *Why?*

PUPPET 2: *Because you promised. Once you do the Promise-Promise-Yes-I-Promise-Pact, then I know that you won't forget.*

PONDER: *If I promise something, I'll do it.*

PUPPET 2: *But how do I know that?*

PONDER: *You don't. You have to trust me.*

PUPPET 2: *I'd rather be sure.*

PONDER: *If you trust me, you can be sure. Can God be trusted to keep all of His promises?*

PUPPET 2: *Definitely.*

PONDER: *Why?*

PUPPET 2: *Because He's always kept all of His promises. He even does the impossible to keep them.*

PONDER: *Have I ever let you down?*

PUPPET 2: *No.*

PONDER: *Have I kept all of my promises?*

PUPPET 2: *Yes.*

PONDER: *Then why do I have to do the Promise-Promise-Yes-I-Promise-Pact?*

PUPPET 2: *Because the fifteenth action in the pact is jumping over the pond. I wanted to see you do that now.*

PONDER: *Then you should have asked. I feel like getting some exercise. Come on. I'll jump over the pond once for you right now.*

(Exit.)

RP8: Finding a Trail

Cast: Ponder the Frog, Noah's Park Puppet 2

Ponder and Puppet 2 move across the stage.

PUPPET 2: *It should be right around here somewhere.*

PONDER: *Are you sure?*

PUPPET 2: *Yeah. It's here. . . . Somewhere . . .*

PONDER: *We should have asked for directions.*

PUPPET 2: *Why do we need directions? I know where we're going. I've been here a million times.*

PONDER: *If you've been here a million times, then why don't you know how to get through these plants?*

PUPPET 2: *Well, maybe not a million times.*

PONDER: *How many?*

PUPPET 2: *That's not important.*

PONDER: *It is to me.*

PUPPET 2: *Fine. I've been here once.*

PONDER: *How long ago?*

PUPPET 2: *Is that really important?*

PONDER: *Yes.*

PUPPET 2: *Fine. A long time ago.*

PONDER: *How long?*

PUPPET 2: *I don't know. I was just a baby.*

PONDER: *(Groans.) I should have known better.*

PUPPET 2: *I do know the way. I've heard my parents tell the story hundreds of times.*

PONDER: *Then that's where we're going.*

PUPPET 2: *Where?*

PONDER: *To your parents for directions.*

PUPPET 2: *Do we have to?*

PONDER: *Yes. God helps boys and girls when they ask, and parents help when we ask. You said that your parents have been here. We're going to ask them.*

PUPPET 2: *I get it. My parents will help us when we ask, just like God helps boys and girls and moms and dads when they ask. That's a great idea. Besides, I'm hungry.*

PONDER: *You just had breakfast.*

PUPPET 2: *I know. It's definitely time for a snack. Let's go. (Exit.)*

RP9: Hiding Out

Cast: Ponder the Frog, Noah's Park Puppet 2

Props: (Optional: potted plant to set on the stage for Puppet 2 to hide behind so he is more visible to the audience)

Puppet 2 is hiding near the side of the stage and peeking its head up repeatedly. Ponder enters.

PONDER: *Is that you, (Puppet 2)?*

PUPPET 2: *Shhh!* (Whispers in a loud stage whisper.) *I don't want anyone to know I'm here.* (Looks all around and ducks halfway back down.)

PONDER: (Softly.) *Why not?*

PUPPET 2: (Softly.) *Animals are looking for me.*

PONDER: (Softly.) *Are you playing hide-and-seek?*

PUPPET 2: (Softly.) *No, it's not a game.*

PONDER: (Softly.) *Are you in trouble?*

PUPPET 2: (Softly.) *Yes.*

PONDER: (Softly.) *I'll help you.*

PUPPET 2: (Softly.) *You can't.*

PONDER: (Softly.) *Is the problem that big?*

PUPPET 2: (Softly.) *No, but you would side with my parents. I'm hiding from them.*

PONDER: *But why? They're great animals.*

PUPPET 2: *They want me to do my chores.*

PONDER: *And you don't want to?*

PUPPET 2: *No. If I do my chores, it'll ruin the whole day.*

PONDER: *So, you're going to stay right here?*

PUPPET 2: *And hide.*

PONDER: *The whole day? (Puppet 2 nods.)* **How long do your chores take to do?**

PUPPET 2: *About 15 minutes.*

PONDER: *So you could do your chores and then play for the rest of the day, or be stuck hiding here for the whole day and not get to play at all.*

(Puppet 2 comes out from its hiding place.)

PUPPET 2: *I didn't think of it like that. I just thought of how tired I am of doing my chores.*

PONDER: *With God's help, you can do a lot more than you think you can.*

PUPPET 2: *Really?*

PONDER: *Definitely.*

PUPPET 2: *What if my chores last for half an hour?*

PONDER: *You still get the rest of the day to play.*

PUPPET 2: *Maybe I should do my chores. I do want to play sometime today.*

PONDER: *Remember Moses? (Puppet 2 nods.)* **Moses tried to get out of doing God's plan, but God wouldn't let him. And I won't let you get out of your parents' plan.**

PUPPET 2: *I knew you'd side with them.*

PONDER: *But it's what you want too, now, isn't it?*

PUPPET 2: *(Sighs.)* **Yes, with God's help, I'm going to do more than I think. Then I'm going to go play.**

PONDER: *Sounds good. See you later,* (name of Puppet 2). *(Both exit to opposite sides.)*

RP10: Whistling Wannabe

Cast: Ponder the Frog, Noah's Park Puppet 2

Props: The sound of someone whistling a song

Ponder and Puppet 2 stand close together.

PUPPET 2: *Like this?* (Puppet 2 tries to whistle, but only the sound of air is heard.)

PONDER: *You're getting closer. Try curling your tongue.*

PUPPET 2: *Like this?* (Puppet 2 tries to whistle, but only the sound of air is heard.)

PONDER: *Almost. Don't breathe so fast.* (Puppet 2 tries to whistle, but only the sound of air is heard.)

PUPPET 2: *Like this?* (Puppet 2 tries to whistle, but only the sound of air is heard.)

PONDER: *Breathe a little faster.* (Puppet 2 tries to whistle, but only the sound of air is heard.)

PUPPET 2: *I give up. I'll never be able to whistle.*

PONDER: *Of course you will.*

PUPPET 2: *I don't have what it takes.*

PONDER: *Do you have a mouth?*

PUPPET 2: *Yes.*

PONDER: *Do you breathe?*

PUPPET 2: *Yes.*

PONDER: *Do you have a tongue?*

PUPPET 2: *Yes.*

PONDER: *Then you have what it takes.*

PUPPET 2: *Then why can't I whistle?*

PONDER: *Some things take practice.*

PUPPET 2: *My friends all know how to whistle.*

PONDER: *Some things come easier to some animals than to others. The question is not what your friends can do but what you can do. Do you want to whistle?*

PUPPET 2: *Yes.*

PONDER: *Then trust that God has given you a mouth that can whistle, and just keep trying. If you keep trying, you'll eventually be able to do it.*

PUPPET 2: *Really?*

PONDER: *Really.*

PUPPET 2: *Like this?* (Puppet 2 tries to whistle, but only the sound of air is heard.)

PONDER: *Trust God, and keep trying.*

(Puppet 2 exits. Suddenly from backstage, the sound of a song being whistled is heard.)

PONDER: *That was great!* (Ponder hurries offstage after Puppet 2.)

RP11: Protection

Cast: Ponder the Frog, Noah's Park Puppet 2

Props: The offstage sound of a crack

Puppet 2 is onstage.

PUPPET 2: *La-dee-da-dee-daaah! Ya-da-da! (Puppet 2 does some wild dancing around the stage as he sings his own off-key music. When he does an especially difficult slide, he hears a crack and stops.)* **Ow! My foot! I hurt my foot! Ow! Ow! Ow! Someone help me. I hurt my foot. Help! Help!**

PONDER: *(Hurries onstage.)* **What's the matter,** *(name of Puppet 2)***?**

PUPPET 2: **I hurt my foot.**

(Ponder goes to Puppet 2 and puts his arm around him to help him take the weight off of his foot.)

PONDER: **Does it hurt?**

PUPPET 2: **Not too bad.**

PONDER: **Is it your right or left foot?**

PUPPET 2: **I don't know.**

PONDER: **Which one hurts?**

PUPPET 2: **I don't know yet.**

PONDER: **What do you mean, you don't know yet?**

PUPPET 2: **I was dancing, and I heard a crack. I must have broken one of my feet.**

(Ponder moves away from Puppet 2.)

PONDER: **Don't be silly. God gives you a way to know if your foot is broken. You'll know because your foot will really hurt.**

(Puppet 2 slowly walks one step forward and then another.)

PUPPET 2: **Neither foot hurts.**

PONDER: **Then you haven't broken either foot. God gives your body many ways to protect itself.**

PUPPET 2: **Really?**

PONDER: **And pain is a way the body tells us to stop doing something or get something fixed.**

PUPPET 2: **God thinks of everything. He provides ways to protect us and save us.** *(Pauses.)* **I wonder what that crack was?**

PONDER: **Probably that tree over there.** *(Both puppets look offstage.)* **It's an old, dead tree, and it's leaning this way.**

PUPPET 2: **If that tree fell, it could have hurt me.** *(There is another sound of a crack.)*

PONDER: **If that tree falls now, it still can hurt you— and me. Let's get out of here!**

(Both puppets run offstage.)

RP12: Clap and Shout

Cast: Ponder the Frog, Noah's Park Puppet 2

Ponder is onstage. Puppet 2 enters.

PUPPET 2: *Ponder, isn't today your birthday?*

PONDER: *Nope.*

PUPPET 2: *Is it an anniversary?*

PONDER: *Nope.*

PUPPET 2: *Did you graduate from anything today?*

PONDER: *Nope.*

PUPPET 2: *Did anything important happen today?*

PONDER: *Nope. Why all the questions?*

PUPPET 2: *I feel happy.*

PONDER: *You feel happy, so you're asking me questions?*

PUPPET 2: *No, I feel happy, so I want to celebrate.*

PONDER: *Well, nothing big happened today.*

PUPPET 2: *I wish it had.*

PONDER: *Nothing big happened, but God gives us reasons to celebrate every day.*

PUPPET 2: *He does?*

PONDER: *Sure. God loves when people celebrate what He has done. Has God done anything for you today?*

PUPPET 2: *He made the sun come up this morning, and now it's warm.*

PONDER: *That's worth celebrating.*

PUPPET 2: *And I did all my chores real fast, and my parents said I did a good job.*

PONDER: *I feel a definite celebration coming on.*

PUPPET 2: *And I came here and met up with you. God gave me a good friend when He made you.*

PONDER: *I'll celebrate that. Woo-hoo! Let's celebrate!*

(Have Puppet 2 and Ponder hop around the stage.)

PUPPET 2: *Yea! Yeah, God! Yippee! Yea! Yea!*

PONDER: *(To kids.)* **Why don't you celebrate with us? When I give the signal, everyone shout out one reason God has given you to celebrate today. It's okay if you all say different things at the same time. God can hear all of them. Are you ready? Go!**

(Let children shout out one reason why they feel like celebrating. If they say it quietly or not at all, have Ponder interact with, "I can't hear you," or "Let's do that again.")

PUPPET 2: **Now those are good reasons to celebrate! Let's clap and shout for God!**

(Let the whole room clap and shout "Yea!" for God as puppets exit.)

RP13: Talking Danger

Cast: Ponder the Frog, Noah's Park Puppet 2

Puppet 2 is onstage. Ponder hurries onstage.

PONDER: *I just heard that an alligator came to the pond. Are you okay?*

PUPPET 2: *Yeah. I was at the pond getting a drink when he lunged at me. I barely had time to climb a tree.*

PONDER: *Did he go after the other animals?*

PUPPET 2: *No. My tree was short. I talked to him—in between the times that he tried to catch and eat me. He came from another swampy pond a long ways from here and was angry at the other animals there. That's why he left. I told him he should forgive them because friendship is important. Then I told him about my family and what I hope to do when I grow up and then . . .*

PONDER: *(Laughs.)* *And while you were talking, the other animals had time to hide.*

PUPPET 2: *I guess so. The alligator started getting angry and told me to be quiet, but what could I do? I was up in a tree. I would have been bored to death if I had had to just sit up there and be quiet. I yelled when he tried to leave me by myself.*

PONDER: *You yelled at him when he left you?*

PUPPET 2: *Yeah. I yelled, "Watch out for the alligator," so no animals would get hurt.*

PONDER: *And that's when he left?*

PUPPET 2: *No, he came back to the tree and told me to be quiet again, but you know me, my mouth runs on and on. Just call me Mr. Talk-and-talk-and-talk—*

PONDER: *When did the alligator leave?*

PUPPET 2: *A little while ago. He said he was going back to where he came from—to get some peace and quiet.*

PONDER: (Laughs.) (Name of Puppet 2), **you just saved the pond and a lot of lives. You used the talent that God has given you.**

PUPPET 2: *What talent?*

PONDER: *Your talent to talk and never stop talking. Today, your talking got rid of a dangerous alligator. Three cheers for* (Name of Puppet 2)*!* (Lead the kids in cheering.) ***Hip, hip, hooray! Hip, hip, hooray! Hip, hip, hooray!***

(Both exit, with Ponder cheering.)

RP14: Growing Strong

Cast: Ponder the Frog, Noah's Park Puppet #2

Puppet 2 is offstage and can be heard grunting and straining as though lifting a heavy object.

PONDER: *What are you doing,* (Name of Puppet 2)*?*

PUPPET 2: *(Offstage.)* **I'm trying** *(grunt)* **to lift these coconut** *(grunt)* **weights.**

PONDER: *(Name of Puppet 2),* **how many coconuts do you have on that broken tree limb?**

PUPPET 2: *Forty-*(grunt)*seven.*

PONDER: *That's way too many for you to be lifting! You could hurt yourself!*

PUPPET 2: *(Enters looking tired.)* **Yeah, I guess you're right, Ponder. Do you know another way I can build muscles?**

PONDER: *Why do you want to build muscles,* (Name of Puppet 2)*?*

PUPPET 2: *Because I'm afraid of spiders.*

PONDER: *And you want to be stronger than a spider?*

PUPPET 2: *Of course not. I'm bigger and stronger than any spider.*

PONDER: *Then why do you need to get stronger?*

PUPPET 2: *I'm afraid to play at the park, because there might be spiders. If I get stronger, then maybe I'll be braver.*

PONDER: *I see. I don't know any other way to make you stronger, but I do know a way to make you braver.*

PUPPET 2: *Is it quicker than lifting coconuts?*

PONDER: *Definitely.*

PUPPET 2: *What is it?*

PONDER: *Believing in God.*

PUPPET 2: *Huh? What does God have to do with this?*

PONDER: *God says we can be strong and brave, because He is with us wherever we go.*

PUPPET 2: *I know He loves and cares for us, but are you sure I don't have to worry about spiders?*

PONDER: *I'll tell you a secret. I used to be afraid of the dark.*

PUPPET 2: *You were? And you're not afraid anymore?*

PONDER: *No. My dad told me that I can trust God to take care of me . . . even in the dark.*

PUPPET 2: *That's great. I'll never have to pick up another coconut. Well, I never really picked up those 47 coconuts. I couldn't lift them.*

PONDER: *Come on,* (Name of Puppet 2). *Let's go to the park!*

(Both exit.)

RP15: All Tied Up

Cast: Ponder the Frog, Noah's Park Puppet #2

Props: Kite string

Puppet 2 is tangled in kite string onstage. Ponder is offstage.

PUPPET 2: *(Shouting.)* **Help! Help! Can anybody help me?**

PONDER: *(Enters.)* **What happened to you,** *(Name of Puppet 2)***?**

PUPPET 2: **I was trying to pull in my kite. It's over there in that tree.**

PONDER: **Do you know how to twirl?**

PUPPET 2: **I don't want to dance. I want to get out of this kite string.**

PONDER: **Do you trust me?**

PUPPET 2: **Yeah.**

PONDER: **Then twirl.** *(Puppet 2 twirls offstage. He reenters, and the string is gone.)*

PUPPET 2: **Thanks, Ponder. Twirling made no sense, but you were right. I twirled out of the kite string. What do you think of my kite?** *(Puppet 2 points offstage.)*

PONDER: **It's a little ways off the ground, but I think it looks cool from here.**

PUPPET 2: **I made it out of bark and branches.**

PONDER: **Bark?**

PUPPET 2: **Sure. If you beat a certain kind of bark long enough, it turns into cloth. It took me six months to make it.**

PONDER: *That's a long time!*

PUPPET 2: *Yeah. My friends thought I was crazy. They didn't think the bark would ever become cloth.*

PONDER: *But you kept doing it, even though what you were doing didn't make sense to your friends, didn't you?*

PUPPET 2: *Yeah. I kept remembering how Noah obeyed God and made the ark, even though what he was doing didn't make any sense.*

PONDER: *You made a great kite.*

PUPPET 2: *Thank you. I have a good friend who likes it, too. So, I share it with him.*

PONDER: *That's nice of you.*

PUPPET 2: *Yeah. I fly my kite for 10 minutes, get it stuck in a tree, and get tangled in the string. Then I go home. My friend, who is a great climber, climbs the tree, gets the kite, flies it, and brings it back to my house. I really like sharing it with him.*

PONDER: *I can see why.*

(Both exit.)

RP16: True Wisdom

Cast: Ponder the Frog, Noah's Park Puppet #2

Props: A stack of books

Puppet 2 is surrounded by books, bent over one of them. Ponder is offstage.

PUPPET 2: *(Muttering at an open book.)* **Abaft. A-B-A-F-T. Abalone** *(pronounced ab-uh-lone-ee)*. **A-B-O-L-O-N-E. No, No, A-B-A-L-O-**

PONDER: *(Enters.)* **Hi,** *(Name of Puppet 2)*. **What are you doing?**

PUPPET 2: **Hi, Ponder. I can't talk right now. I'm memorizing all of these books. Abalone. A-B-A-L-O-N-E.**

PONDER: **You're going to know a lot of stuff if you memorize everything in those books.**

PUPPET 2: **I don't care about that.**

PONDER: **Then why are you memorizing them?**

PUPPET 2: **I want to be wise.**

PONDER: **You don't get wisdom from books. You get knowledge.**

PUPPET 2: **Are you sure?**

PONDER: **Yeah. There's only one way to be wise.**

PUPPET 2: **Are you sure?**

PONDER: **Absolutely. You get wisdom from asking God what to do.**

PUPPET 2: **Are you sure?**

PONDER: **Yes. He knows what's best for you.**

PUPPET 2: **Are you sure?**

PONDER: *Why do you keep asking me that?*

PUPPET 2: *In one of these books, it said—* (Stands up tall with head cocked proudly to one side.) *— that if I ask questions and stand like this, people will think I'm wise.*

PONDER: *I should have known. Well, it looks like you have a choice.*

PUPPET 2: *Are you sure?*

PONDER: *You can look like you're wise, or you can actually be wise.*

PUPPET 2: *Yeah. You're right. I want to be wise, not just look like I am. I think I'll start by asking God what He wants me to do.*

PONDER: *Great choice.*

(Exit.)

RP17: Big and Small

Cast: Ponder the Frog, Noah's Park Puppet #2

Puppet 2 is onstage.

PONDER: *(Enters.)* **Hey,** *(Name of Puppet 2)***, want to play How-High-Can-You-Jump with me?**

PUPPET 2: **No, thanks.**

PONDER: **How about How-Loud-Can-You-Ribbit?**

PUPPET 2: **No, thanks.**

PONDER: **How about How-Quiet-Can-You-Hide?**

PUPPET 2: **I don't feel like playing a game.**

PONDER: **What's wrong? Are you sick? Did you hurt yourself? What's the matter? You always want to play.**

PUPPET 2: **I don't feel like it today. Look.** *(Points upward and offstage.)* **That's my new kite. It's in the tree. My friend is gone for a few days, or he could have gotten it down easily. I'll never be able to get it down by myself.**

PONDER: **God cares about all our problems. He's always ready to help.**

PUPPET 2: **Not this problem.**

PONDER: *What do you mean, "Not this problem"?*

PUPPET 2: *God has a lot of really big things to do. He has to keep the moon and stars in the sky. He has to make sure that the sun sets at the right time and rises every morning. He's in charge of the whole world. Getting a kite out of a tree is a pretty small job.*

PONDER: *So?*

PUPPET 2: *I think He's very busy. He might be tired.*

PONDER: *(Name of Puppet 2),* **God IS in charge of all of those things. But He doesn't get tired. He cares about the little things too.**

PUPPET 2: *He does? He cares that my kite is stuck in the tree?*

PONDER: *Yes, (Name of Puppet 2),* **He even cares about that.**

PUPPET 2: *That's great! God is ready to help with all our big and small problems—even with my kite! He can send the wind to blow it out of the tree, get another animal to reach it, or . . .*

PONDER: *God can do a lot of things. All you have to do is ask Him.*

(Exit.)

RP18: Pay Attention

Cast: Ponder the Frog, Noah's Park Puppet #2

Ponder is onstage beginning to chat with the kids. Puppet 2 runs onstage.

PONDER: *What's the matter?*

PUPPET 2: *Nothing. I forgot what you said. Do I take a right or do I take a left when I get to the moss-colored rock?*

PONDER: *You take a right.*

PUPPET 2: *Okay. Thanks, Ponder.*

PONDER: *You're welcome. (Puppet 2 runs offstage.) It's a beautiful day today. Are you having a good day, kids? (Let kids respond.)*

PUPPET 2: *(Enters at a run.) Do I jump over or go under the dead tree after I take a right at the moss-colored rock?*

PONDER: *Jump over it.*

PUPPET 2: *Thanks, Ponder.*

PONDER: *You're welcome. (Puppet 2 runs offstage.) I like sitting here in the sun. Are any of you doing anything special today? (Let kids respond.)*

PUPPET 2: *(Enters at a run.) Ponder, do I go through or around the waterfall after I jump over the dead tree that is to the right of the moss-colored rock?*

PONDER: *(Name of Puppet 2), you didn't pay attention to my directions, did you?*

PUPPET 2: *No, I didn't, and now I'm really, really tired. If I'd listened closely the first time, I'd already be eating those pomegranates you found.*

PONDER: *I hope you pay better attention to God's directions than you do mine. To pay attention, you have to stop what you're doing and listen.*

PUPPET 2: *I know, but that game of gruberpyle was so much fun. I didn't want to stop playing to listen! From now on, though, I'm going to pay attention when people give me directions.*

PONDER: *Good idea. Do you want me to give you the directions to the pomegranates one more time?*

PUPPET 2: *I do.*

PONDER: *Jump over the big tree to the right of the moss-colored rock. Then go around the waterfall, and you'll find pomegranates next to an enormous bush.*

PUPPET 2: *Got it. Thanks, Ponder.* (Puppet 2 exits.)

PONDER: *Kids, if you pay attention to God's directions as well as* (Name of Puppet 2) *just listened to mine, you will always find what you need.*

(Exit.)

RP19: The Right Choices

Cast: Ponder the Frog, Noah's Park Puppet #2

Ponder and Puppet 2 are onstage.

PUPPET 2: *Hey Ponder, want to paint signs with me?*

PONDER: *What are the signs for, (Name of Puppet 2)?*

PUPPET 2: *For the animal bash game on Saturday. You know, when the Mashed Potatoes play against the Turkeys. I'm making signs that say, "Go Mashed Potatoes" and "The Potatoes are going to cream you!"*

PONDER: *(Laughing.) I guess you want everyone to know that you are cheering for the Mashed Potatoes.*

PUPPET 2: *That's right. I might even make spitballs to shoot at the Turkey fans. Do you want to help?*

PONDER: *Sure, I'll help you paint signs. But no spitballs.*

PUPPET 2: *Great. I wish I was on a team like the Mashed Potatoes.*

PONDER: *You are. You're on God's team.*

PUPPET 2: *Yeah, but it's not like I get to go around and tell everyone that I'm on His team.*

PONDER: *Why not? God wants you to tell others.*

PUPPET 2: *He does? I didn't know that. Maybe when I get done with the signs for the Mashed Potatoes, I should paint some for Him.*

PONDER: *If you want to paint a sign, that's fine, but it's not necessary.*

PUPPET 2: *Of course it's necessary. How will animals know I'm on God's team if I don't carry a sign?*

PONDER: *You show others that you're on His team by the choices you make.*

PUPPET 2: *Oh.*

PONDER: *If you follow His rules and treat others well, then you're making good choices.*

PUPPET 2: *So, maybe I shouldn't make spitballs to shoot at the Turkey fans. I want to show others that I'm on God's team.*

PONDER: *Good idea.*

PUPPET 2: *Okay, no spitballs. I'll cheer for the Mashed Potatoes, but I'll make sure my choices show that I am following God.*

PONDER: *Great idea. Now, let's go make those Mashed Potatoes signs!*

(Both exit.)

RP20: God's Power

Cast: Ponder the Frog, Noah's Park Puppet #2

Ponder and Puppet 2 are onstage.

PUPPET 2: *(Moaning and groaning as if in pain.)* **Ohhhh! Ohhhh! Ponder, I think I have a rare form of chicken pox. My stomach hurts so badly.**

PONDER: *(Name of Puppet 2),* **chicken pox isn't a stomach disease. When you have chicken pox, you get itchy red bumps all over your body.**

PUPPET 2: *(Stops moaning.)* **Oh.** *(Waits a few seconds and then starts moaning again.)* **Ponder, I think I have the rabbit-tongue measles.**

PONDER: *(Name of Puppet 2),* **you don't have the rabbit-tongue measles. Only rabbits get that disease.**

PUPPET 2: *(Stops moaning.)* **Oh, yeah.** *(Starts moaning again.)* **Ponder, I think I have Australian caterpillar disease.**

PONDER: **Australian caterpillar disease? What's that?**

PUPPET 2: *(Stops moaning.)* **It's a really bad disease, one where you get really sick, and you can't help clean old elephants.**

PONDER: **Is it your turn to help give Old Elephant a bath?**

PUPPET 2: **Yes. Tomorrow. My mom says that unless I'm sick, I have to do it. I'm scared. Old Elephant is so big.**

PONDER: **Old Elephant is big, but God's power is bigger. Nothing is too difficult for God.**

PUPPET 2: *Nothing? Are you sure God's power is strong enough to help me clean Old Elephant?*

PONDER: *There aren't any problems too big for God. Remember, your mother wouldn't ask you to do something that would hurt you.*

PUPPET 2: *I didn't think of it that way.*

PONDER: *Did you know that Old Elephant tells really good stories?*

PUPPET 2: *No. Maybe this won't be so bad after all.*

PONDER: *Even if you get scared again, just remember that God is greater than your biggest problem.*

PUPPET 2: *I will. Thanks, Ponder.*

(Exit.)

RP21: Seeing Clearly

Cast: Ponder the Frog, Noah's Park Puppet #2

Props: A pair of glasses

Puppet 2 wears glasses and bumps into things. Ponder enters.

PONDER:	*(Name of Puppet 2)*, **I didn't know you wore glasses.**
PUPPET 2:	**Ponder, is that you?** *(He bumps into Ponder.)* **Oh, hi.**
PONDER:	**When did our animal doctor prescribe glasses for you?**
PUPPET 2:	**He didn't.** *(Puppet 2 bumps into something.)*
PONDER:	**They don't seem to be helping you. Why are you wearing them?**
PUPPET 2:	**Because I'm not green or wise like you.**
PONDER:	**When you get to be my age, you could be even wiser. But what does that have to do with your glasses?**
PUPPET 2:	**Other animals don't pay attention to me like they do you, but now they will. I have glasses just like you.**
PONDER:	**Are you jealous of me?**
PUPPET 2:	**Jealous?**
PONDER:	**Yes. Are you upset that sometimes your friends give me more attention than they give you?**
PUPPET 2:	**Of course not, but it would be nice if they listened to me just a little bit.**
PONDER:	**Don't be jealous of me. God created you to be the way He wanted you to be. He'll give you everything you need.**

PUPPET 2: *Are you sure?*

PONDER: *Yes. No matter where you go or what you do, there will always be someone smarter or prettier or nicer than you. So instead of comparing yourself to them, you should work to become a better you.*

PUPPET 2: *I can do that.*

PONDER: *I know you can. You don't need those glasses to be someone you're not.*

PUPPET 2: *What a relief. Thank you, Ponder. And don't worry. I'll put your glasses back on your lily pad.*

PONDER: *Those are my glasses?*

PUPPET 2: *Yes. But now that I know I can trust God and not be jealous of you, you can have them back.* (Exits.)

PONDER: *Oh my. I need a new prescription. I didn't even recognize my own glasses.*

(Exits.)

RP22: The Best Kind of Friend

Cast: Ponder the Frog, Noah's Park Puppet #2

Puppet 2 is onstage.

PUPPET 2: *Oh no, you go first. (Pause.) Oh no, after you. (Pause.) By all means, you go first. (Ponder enters.) It's definitely your turn first.*

PONDER: *What are you doing,* (Name of Puppet 2)?

PUPPET 2: *Practicing.*

PONDER: *Practicing what?*

PUPPET 2: *Practicing to be my new baby brother's best friend.*

PONDER: *A best friend is an unselfish friend.*

PUPPET 2: *Exactly. If my brother is thirsty, I'm not going to drink all the water in the pond before he takes a drink.*

PONDER: *Taking turns is unselfish.*

PUPPET 2: *If we jump on the rocks over the waterfall together, I'm going to let him hop on the biggest rocks.*

PONDER: *Letting him have good things is unselfish.*

PUPPET 2: *Then I can be his best friend and stop sharing my parents with him.*

PONDER: *What do you mean?*

PUPPET 2: *I want to be his best friend, but I don't like how he takes my parents from me. My mom used to wake me up first in the morning, but now she feeds my brother first. At lunch, my dad plays with both of us, not just me anymore. And at night, both of my parents used to tell me stories. Now only one does.*

PONDER: *Your parents are your brother's parents too.*

PUPPET 2:   *No way.*

PONDER: *They are going to be his parents for his whole life.*

PUPPET 2:   *You mean I have to share them with him forever?*

PONDER: *Yeah.*

PUPPET 2:   *Oh. Oh well. I guess it'll only make me a better friend if I share them, too.*

PONDER: *A best friend is an unselfish friend.*

PUPPET 2:   *You're right. Hey, if I share my parents with him, I can share everything with him. This could be really good. I can share my chores, my mistakes, my problems, everything.*

PONDER: *One step at a time, (Name of Puppet 2). One step at a time.*

        (Exit.)

RP23: The Best Way

Cast: Ponder the Frog and Noah's Park Puppet 2

Puppet 2 is onstage. Ponder enters.

PUPPET 2: *Careful! Don't fall in the hole!*

PONDER: *(Jumps to the side.)* **Thanks for warning me. I wouldn't have known it was there. It's covered with leaves.**

PUPPET 2: *Yeah. It's a trap. After Someone-I-don't-want-to-name falls into it, I'll fill it up so no one else gets hurt.*

PONDER: **Are you getting even with someone?**

PUPPET 2: *Yeah. This Someone-I-don't-want-to-name has been annoying me for weeks.*

PONDER: **I wouldn't do that if I were you. God's way is always better than getting even.**

PUPPET 2: *Wait until you hear. Yesterday, he climbed a tree and dropped leaves on me.*

PONDER: **That wasn't nice.**

PUPPET 2: *The day before, he pulled back a branch and hit me in the face.*

PONDER: **Animals can be mean. Last week, someone yanked my lily pad out from under me while I was in midair. I landed in the water with a splash instead of on my pad.**

PUPPET 2: *That's awful. What did you do?*

PONDER: **I asked him to join me for lunch.**

PUPPET 2: *What? Why did you do that?*

PONDER: **God said to turn the other cheek if someone does something mean. He also said to treat others the same way we want to be treated.**

PUPPET 2:   *Did you really have lunch with him?*

PONDER: *Yes, and he hasn't annoyed me since. As a matter of fact, we've had lunch together a couple of times since then.*

PUPPET 2:   *Maybe God's way IS better than getting even. You've got a friend now instead of someone who annoys you. If I do it God's way, I've got a lot of work ahead of me.*

PONDER: *Doing things God's way isn't easy, but it is worth it.*

PUPPET 2:   *I agree, but I wasn't talking about that. I was talking about the hole. I have to fill it with dirt before anyone gets hurt.*

PONDER: *I'll help. Let's go get our shovels.*

(Both exit.)

RP24: Muddy Days

Cast: Ponder the Frog and Noah's Park Puppet 2

Ponder is onstage looking ill (drooping and with scrunched-up mouth). Puppet 2 enters.

PUPPET 2: *(Talking to self.)* **What a horrible day.** *(Puppet 2 stops and stares at Ponder.)* **What happened to you, Ponder? You look awful.**

PONDER: *I feel awful.*

PUPPET 2: *Did you get stuck in that rainstorm this morning?*

PONDER: *Yes. When the wind started blowing, I hid under an enormous leaf.*

PUPPET 2: *That wasn't so bad.*

PONDER: *No, it wasn't, but then the leaf bent, and all the water it was holding fell on me.*

PUPPET 2: *But you like water.*

PONDER: *I do, but there was so much water that it swept me out into the open field. I got stuck in the mud.*

PUPPET 2: *But you like mud.*

PONDER: *I do, but the wildebeests started to stampede, and I was stuck right in their way. I barely made it out of the mud alive.*

PUPPET 2: *That's awful.*

PONDER: *By the time I got out of their way, I had so much mud on me that a wild pig tried to wallow in me. He shoved me against a tree twice before he realized I wasn't a walking mud puddle.*

PUPPET 2: *Oh dear, no wonder you look awful. What did you do after all that?*

PONDER: *I talked to God.*

PUPPET 2: *You did what?*

PONDER: *Life isn't always fun, and it isn't always easy. Whenever life gets tough, I talk to God.*

PUPPET 2: *What does that do?*

PONDER: *God knows how to get me out of my problems or how to help me live through them.*

PUPPET 2: *I see. Maybe I need to talk to God too. My little brother was up all night last night crying. I couldn't sleep. Now I feel awful.*

PONDER: *Talk to God. He'll help you get through it.*

PUPPET 2: *(Yawns.)* *Great idea. I think I will. Then I'm going to take a nap. I'm tired.*

(Exit.)

RP25: The Real Winner

Cast: Ponder the Frog and Noah's Park Puppet 2

Props: A small medal

Puppet 2 is onstage wearing the medal.

PUPPET 2: *Hey kids, look at my medal! Isn't it cool?*
(Ponder enters.)

PONDER: *Did I hear something about a medal?*

PUPPET 2: *You sure did. Look at my medal, Ponder.*

PONDER: *(Examines the medal closely.)* **Wow,** *(Name of Puppet 2),* **it says, "First Place"! Did you win it in a race?**

PUPPET 2: *No.*

PONDER: *For some other sport?*

PUPPET 2: *No.*

PONDER: *For eating the most food in a contest?*

PUPPET 2: *No.*

PONDER: *For saying the most Bible verses?*

PUPPET 2: *No.*

PONDER: *Was it an art contest?*

PUPPET 2: *No.*

PONDER: *I give up. What did you win the medal for?*

PUPPET 2: *Nothing. I didn't win it.*

PONDER: *Then whose is it?*

PUPPET 2: *My dad's. He gave it to me.*

PONDER: *So your dad gave you his medal to play with? Maybe you shouldn't call it your medal.*

PUPPET 2: *But it is my medal. My dad gave it to me, but he earned it.*

PONDER: *Interesting. You are giving your dad credit for winning the medal that you own. That's how God wants us to treat Him. He wants us to give Him credit for the good things that happen to us.*

PUPPET 2: *That makes sense. When good things happen to us, it's because God has given them to us, just like my dad gave me his medal.*

PONDER: *What did your dad do to get that medal?*

PUPPET 2: *I don't know.*

PONDER: *Let's go ask him.*

PUPPET 2: *Okay. If I were giving my dad a medal, the medal would be for being the best dad in the world.*

PONDER: *That might be why he gave the medal to you. He thinks you're pretty great too.*

PUPPET 2: *Really?*

PONDER: *Yeah, fathers give good things to their children, and they love it when their children give them credit for those things. Let's go talk to your dad.*

(Exit together.)

RP26: Getting Wisdom

Cast: Ponder the Frog, Noah's Park Puppet 2, Park Patrol Kid

Ponder is onstage. Puppet 2 and PPK rush on. PPK stands next to or behind the stage, interacting.

PUPPET 2: *(With urgency.)* **Ponder! We're looking for a leaf with orange on top and blue on the bottom.**

PPK: **Yeah, can you help us?**

PONDER: **I haven't seen one like that.**

PUPPET 2: **It's an emergency.**

PONDER: **I'll help you find it.** *(Starts looking around on the ground.)* **What happened?**

PPK: **It's complicated.**

PONDER: **Complicated? Who is the leaf for?**

PPK: **Me.**

PONDER: **You? Are you okay?**

PUPPET 2: **He will be once we find an altoidemingo plant.**

PONDER: *(Keeps looking.)* **Do you need the leaf for homework or something?**

PUPPET 2: **No. Here it is.**

PONDER: **That's not orange. That's a faded red.**

PPK: **You're right.**

PONDER: **So you don't have to learn about the leaf?**

PPK: **No, I have to rub it between my hands while standing on a large stack of bamboo sticks on a Tuesday when the moon is full and say, "I am as wise as Solomon," 12 times.**

(Ponder stops looking for the plant.)

PONDER: *You what?*

PUPPET 2: *He has to rub it betwe—*

PONDER: *I heard the first time. Why would you do that?*

PUPPET 2: *He (she) wants to get Solomon's wisdom. I heard some salamanders discussing it.*

PONDER: *You don't need to do that. If you want wisdom, all you have to do is ask.*

PPK: *Can I get some wisdom from you?*

PONDER: *Don't ask ME. God has all the wisdom in the world. He said that if you ask Him for it, He'll give it to you.*

PPK: *Really? (Ponder nods.) That's great. I'm going to go home and ask Him for wisdom right now. Oh wait. That won't work.*

PONDER: *God gives wisdom to those who ask.*

PUPPET 2: *We understand that, but what are we going to do with all the bamboo rods we gathered?*

PONDER: *While you're asking God for wisdom, you might want to ask Him about that, too.*

(Puppet 2 and PPK look at each other and nod.)

PPK: *Good idea. I've got a LOT I need to talk to God about.*

(Exit.)

RP27: What to Do

Cast: Ponder the Frog, Noah's Park Puppet 2, Park Patrol Kid (same as in RP 26)

Puppet 2 and Park Patrol Kid are onstage chatting. Ponder walks by.

PONDER: *Did you ask God for wisdom?*

PPK: *I did. But I have to tell you, I don't feel any different.*

PONDER: *Why would you feel different?*

PPK: *I don't know. I expected lightning to strike me or the air to grow cold.*

PUPPET 2: *I expected that at LEAST the sun would stop shining for a few minutes. But nothing happened.*

PONDER: *Sometimes God works that way, but He also works through natural things.*

PPK: *I don't think He worked through me at all.*

PONDER: *We'll see. By the way, whatever happened to that enormous stack of bamboo sticks?*

PUPPET 2: *We could have used God's wisdom for that one. We had stacked them where my family sleeps. It took me all day to move them.*

PONDER: *Where did you put them?*

PPK: *I suddenly got the idea that I could put them by those two big rocks beside the big waterfall.*

PONDER: *That was wise. They would stop the water from splashing drinking animals.*

PPK: *That's what I thought.*

PONDER: *So that's where you put them?*

PPK: *Not all of them. As I was moving them, I noticed that a few little monkeys needed help climbing the big tree. I leaned two sticks against the tree so they could quickly climb up and down.*

PONDER: *That was wise.*

PPK: *Then there were a few birds looking for twigs. I crushed one into small pieces for them.*

PONDER: *It looks like God answered your prayer.*

PPK: *No, He didn't.*

PONDER: *Did you know what to do with the bamboo sticks before you asked Him for wisdom?*

PPK: *No, I got the idea right after I asked Him.*

PONDER: *He gave you the wisdom you needed to move those sticks.*

PUPPET 2: *You're right!* (Name of PPK) *asked for wisdom, and God showed him* (her) *how to do what was needed. Wow! God's amazing!*

(Exit.)

RP28: Secret Valley

Cast: Ponder the Frog and Noah's Park Puppet 2

Ponder and Puppet 2 are walking together.

PUPPET 2: *How long have you known about it?*

PONDER: *Noah showed it to me shortly after we left the ark.*

PUPPET 2: *You've known about this secret valley that long? Why didn't you tell me?*

PONDER: *I would have if I had thought you were interested.*

PUPPET 2: *I AM interested. I am very interested. I love secret valleys.*

PONDER: *How many secret valleys do you know?*

PUPPET 2: *None, but I'm going to love it.*

PONDER: *Okay, it's right here.*

PUPPET 2: *But I come here all the time. I eat my lunch here. Where is it?*

PONDER: *Look for it. It's worth searching for.*

PUPPET 2: *(Looks up high and down low.)* *I don't see anything but a rock and a tree. The tree is so close to the rock that I can't get around it. And the rock is so big, I can't get over it.*

PONDER: *Look at where the rock and tree come together. Slide between them.*

PUPPET 2: *But why? There's a dead-end rock on the other side.*

PONDER: *Just do what I say.*

PUPPET 2: *Okay. (Puppet 2 slides offstage.)* **Wow. Oh wow. It's a gateway to the secret valley. Wow! That valley is gorgeous.**

PONDER: **It is. And you can't see it until you're on the other side of that tree. On this side it looks like a dead end.**

PUPPET 2: *(Reenters.)* **That valley looks amazing.**

PONDER: **I think it's a secret because of the way this rock juts out. It hides the entrance from view.**

PUPPET 2: **Unbelievable. You opened the way to this valley, and it's amazing!**

PONDER: **I like how you said that. It reminds me of how Jesus opened the way to God.**

PUPPET 2: **I know that God is more amazing than this valley, but wow oh wow!**

PONDER: **And once we go through Jesus, we know that God is worthy of praise, just like you're full of awe for the valley.**

PUPPET 2: **Can we go into it?**

PONDER: **Sure. You first. I'll be right behind you.**

(Both slide offstage.)

RP29: U-Turn

Cast: Ponder the Frog and Puppet 2

Ponder and Puppet 2 enter. Puppet 2 holds its head at an odd angle and moans.

PUPPET 2: *My neck hurts so bad.*

PONDER: *We can stand here to watch the Mashed Potatoes play the Turkeys.*

PUPPET 2: *I can't see the field. All I can see is the scoreboard.*

PONDER: *Try to turn your body this way.* (Puppet 2 turns so he can see the field.)

PUPPET 2: *There they are. That's the whistle for the game. If I stay like this, I should be able to see the whole game.* (There is a crash offstage. Ponder turns to look.)

PONDER: *What was that?*

PUPPET 2: *I don't know. All I can see is the field. Yeah! The Mashed Potatoes scored. Go, Mashed Potatoes!*

PONDER: *Oh.* (Ponder turns to the field.) *I missed that score. I was looking behind us. I don't know what that sound was.* (There is another crash offstage. Ponder turns to look.)

PUPPET 2: *What's happening?*

PONDER: *I don't know. I can't see anything that could have made that sound.*

PUPPET 2: *Yeah! The Mashed Potatoes scored again.* (Ponder turns back to the field.) *One more score, and they win.*

PONDER: *That was quick. I missed it again.* (An even louder crash is heard offstage. Ponder turns to look.)

Lesson R29: Don' t Let Anything Turn You From God | **RP・63**

PUPPET 2: *The Mashed Potatoes win! I knew they would. That was a great animal bash.*

PONDER: *What?* (Ponder turns back to the field.) *It's over? I didn't even get to see a single score.*

PUPPET 2: *They were great. I guess you should have kept your eyes on the field.*

PONDER: *You're right. You know, that crick in your neck helped you see the whole game. You couldn't turn your head, so you kept your eyes on the field. I know that I shouldn't let anything turn me from God, but I didn't know that I shouldn't let anything turn me from watching the game. The next time we come to an animal bash, I'm going to remember that!*

(Both exit.)

RP30: The Ditch

Cast: Ponder the Frog and Puppet 2

Ponder and Puppet 2 are walking.

PUPPET 2: *No, I haven't taken this path for two years. I think that that there has to be—(Puppet 2 drops down below the stage as if he has fallen into a ditch.)*

PONDER: *Where did you go?*

PUPPET 2: *(Offstage.) I'm down here.*

PONDER: *(Looks around and then looks down.) Oh. What are you doing down there?*

PUPPET 2: *(Offstage.) I fell into a hole.*

PONDER: *That's a big hole.*

PUPPET 2: *(Offstage.) It's gigantic.*

PONDER: *Can you get out?*

PUPPET 2: *(Offstage.) Yeah, but it's going to take me a minute. I put steps over here, so I could get out.*

PONDER: *You put steps there? When did you have time to do that? You just fell into the hole.*

PUPPET 2: *(Offstage.) I didn't make them today. I made them about two years ago when I dug this hole.*

PONDER: *You dug this hole.*

PUPPET 2: *(Offstage.) Yeah, and then I covered it with leaves so no one would see it.*

PONDER: *Why didn't you fill it in when you were done?*

PUPPET 2: (Slowly Puppet 2's face and then body appear as if he is climbing up steps.) **I meant to. I just never got around to it. I guess digging ditches and leaving them has consequences.**

PONDER: **You're right. Open ditches are a lot like sin. Sin always has consequences and so do open ditches.**

PUPPET 2: **I'm going to fill this one in this afternoon. I'm glad the leaves were still on this ditch. That means that no one else ever fell into it.** (Puppet 2 moves to the side and drops down as if he dropped into another hole.)

PONDER: (Looks around.) **Where did you go this time?**

PUPPET 2: (Offstage.) **I'm down here. I forgot. I dug two ditches, but I don't have stairs for this one. Can you help me get out?**

PONDER: **Sure, let me get a vine. There aren't any more holes around here, are there?**

PUPPET 2: **No, at least I don't think so.**

(Ponder drops down as if he fell into a hole.)

PONDER: **I'm pretty sure you dug three ditches.**

(End.)

RP31: Glad You' re Here

Cast: Ponder the Frog and Puppet 2

Ponder is onstage. Puppet 2 enters.

PONDER: *(Name of Puppet 2),* **you're just the animal that I need.**

PUPPET 2: **Really? Why?**

PONDER: **I have to figure out the exact color of that leaf. I can't see it so well even with my glasses, but you have young, healthy eyes. Can you tell me what color it is?**

PUPPET 2: *(Puppet 2 looks into the audience as if studying a plant.)* **It's a blue-green color with little orange flecks on it.**

PONDER: **Perfect. That's exactly what I needed to know. My job's finished.**

PUPPET 2: **Glad I could help.**

PONDER: **So am I.** *(Name of a Leader)* **asked me to learn everything I could about this plant. I didn't know what to do, so I trusted God for the help I needed.**

PUPPET 2: **And I came along.**

PONDER: **True, but first a little caterpillar came along and told me how it tasted.**

PUPPET 2: **And then I came along.**

PONDER: **True, but after the caterpillar, a bird told me how it looked from the sky.**

PUPPET 2: **And then I came along.**

PONDER: **True, but after the bird, another friend came along and told me that she sleeps on plants like these because they're really soft.**

PUPPET 2: *When did I come along?*

PONDER: *Right after that friend, you came along to help me figure out its color. Now I can go and tell* (Name of Leader) *everything I know about this plant.*

PUPPET 2: *Can I come too?*

PONDER: *Sure. You can help make the time go by faster as I walk over to find* (Name of Leader). *You see, God always provides the exact help I need.*

(Exit.)

RP32: God Listens

Cast: Ponder the Frog and Puppet 2

Ponder leans against the edge of the stage, relaxing, as if asleep.
Puppet 2 hurries onstage.

PUPPET 2: *Ponder! Ponder! Wait until you hear what happened. I was walking on the path to the secret valley when suddenly a herd of elephants came crashing through the trees. I dodged one, then another, then another. I would have climbed a tree, but they were knocking them down. I finally got away from them. I was running so fast that I fell into the pond. Just then . . . hey, wait a minute, are you even listening? Ponder? Did you hear what I said? No one ever listens to me, even when I've had an amazing adventure.*

PONDER: *I heard what you said.*

PUPPET 2: *You're just saying that.*

PONDER: *No. I heard every word.*

PUPPET 2: *Sure you did. Then tell me what happened.*

PONDER: *You were going to the secret valley when you were almost run down by a herd of elephants. You dodged out of their way, but then fell into the pond.*

PUPPET 2: *You did hear what I said.*

PONDER: *I told you I did.*

PUPPET 2: *I know, but it felt like you weren't listening.*

PONDER: *Sometimes, that's how people feel about God, but God always hears what people say when they pray to Him.*

PUPPET 2: *I'm sorry, Ponder. I should have trusted you.*

PONDER: *That's okay. Now go on with your story. Even if I don't "ooooo" and "ahhhhh" at every exciting point, it doesn't mean I'm not listening.*

PUPPET 2: *God listens when I pray, and you listen too. That's great!*

(Exit.)

RP33: Number One

Cast: Ponder the Frog and Puppet 2

Ponder is onstage. Puppet 2 enters, hopping as he cheers.

PUPPET 2: *We're number one! We're number one!*

PONDER: *So, the Mashed Potatoes won their game, again.*

PUPPET 2: *They did. They were so amazing. They're definitely number one.*

PONDER: *Like the sun?*

PUPPET 2: *I don't know what you mean.*

PONDER: *There's only one sun. So, the Mashed Potatoes are a team that stands alone like the sun.*

PUPPET 2: *There are other suns.*

PONDER: *True, but they're all far away. There's only one sun for our planet.*

PUPPET 2: *I get it. There are other teams, but the Mashed Potatoes are a team that stands alone. They're like a pond.*

PONDER: *There are other ponds.*

PUPPET 2: *I know, but there's only one pond that we use.*

PONDER: *True. I guess you could say that the Mashed Potatoes are like Noah.*

PUPPET 2: *There are other people.*

PONDER: *True, but only one Noah who listened to God, built an ark, and saved all our lives.*

PUPPET 2: *You're right. The Mashed Potatoes are like God.*

PONDER: *I don't think so. There are other teams.*

PUPPET 2: *Sure. And there are other gods . . . wait a minute. Are there any other gods?*

PONDER: *No, not real ones. There's only one God.*

PUPPET 2: *Oh, I see. He's not like anything or anyone else, because He's in a class of His own.*

PONDER: *Exactly. The Mashed Potatoes are good, but they aren't like God. There are no other gods—even though some people make some up. God is the one and only God.*

PUPPET 2: *You're right. He is a team of His own, one that I definitely want to be on.*

PONDER: *Good choice.*

PUPPET 2: *God's number one! God's number one! Come on, kids, say it with me. God's number one! God's number one!*

(Puppets exit to the chants of "God's number one!")

RP34: God Cares

Cast: Ponder the Frog and Puppet 2

Ponder is onstage. Puppet 2 enters.

PUPPET 2: *Hi, Ponder. Do you need help with anything?*

PONDER: *No, thanks.*

PUPPET 2: *Can I get you some water? Are you thirsty?*

PONDER: *No.*

PUPPET 2: *Are you hungry? I can find some flies for you to eat.*

PONDER: *No, I just ate.*

PUPPET 2: *There has to be something I can do for you.*

PONDER: *Why do you want to do something for me? You're not usually so helpful.*

PUPPET 2: *I feel awful about the picnic.*

PONDER: *What picnic?* (Puppet 2 covers his mouth with his hands.)

PUPPET 2: *I wasn't supposed to say anything.* (Hangs his head.) *I might as well tell you. We're having a large animal picnic by the pond tomorrow, and I didn't send you an invitation. I am so sorry.*

PONDER: *I had forgotten about the animal picnic.*

PUPPET 2: *We have it every year. I don't know why you weren't invited. I wish I could change it, but everything's set now.*

PONDER: *Don't feel bad.*

PUPPET 2: *You're being nice to me when you should be yelling at me. You even care for me when I feel bad.*

PONDER: *I do care for you, just like God cares for you when you feel bad, but . . .*

PUPPET 2: *No, don't say anything else. I can't take it. I feel so guilty.*

PONDER: *What I'm trying to say . . .*

PUPPET 2: *I know. I need to do something about it.*

PONDER: *That's nice of you, but . . .*

PUPPET 2: *Okay. You can have my invitation.*

PONDER: *Stop! Let me speak. The reason I wasn't invited is because I won't be here for it. I'm visiting my sister at the next pond over.*

PUPPET 2: *Oh.*

PONDER: *I told the person in charge not to send me an invitation.*

PUPPET 2: *Oh.*

PONDER: *Okay?*

PUPPET 2: *Okay. Can I take my invitation back then?*

(End.)

RP35: Just Like You

Cast: Ponder the Frog and Puppet 2

Ponder and Puppet 2 enter.

PONDER:	**What a beautiful day.** *(Ponder looks around.)*
PUPPET 2:	**What a beautiful day.** *(Puppet 2 looks around.)*
PONDER:	**The sky is blue.** *(Ponder looks up.)*
PUPPET 2:	**The sky is blue.** *(Puppet 2 looks up.)*
PONDER:	**The leaves are green.** *(Ponder looks to one side.)*
PUPPET 2:	**The leaves are green.** *(Puppet 2 looks to the same side.)*
PONDER:	**The air is warm.** *(Ponder basks in the sun.)*
PUPPET 2:	**The air is warm.** *(Puppet 2 basks in the sun.)*
PONDER:	*(Name of Puppet 2)***, why are you repeating everything I say and doing what I do?**
PUPPET 2:	**Why are you—**
PONDER:	**Stop! Answer my question.**
PUPPET 2:	**Oh, okay. I want to be more like God.**
PONDER:	**That doesn't answer my question. Why are you following me?**
PUPPET 2:	**I'm following you, because sometimes I see you do the same things that** *(Name of Leader)* **does.**
PONDER:	**It's true I do some of the same things that** *(Name of Leader)* **does, but that still doesn't answer my question.**
PUPPET 2:	**It's obvious.** *(Name of Leader)* **follows God. You follow** *(Name of Leader)***. I'm following you.**
PONDER:	**Oh, I see. You're trying to learn from those who follow God.**

PUPPET 2: *Exactly. (Name of Leader) lives too far away for me to follow him, but you don't.*

PONDER: *That's smart, but you don't have to follow every action and say every word.*

PUPPET 2: *Are you sure? What am I supposed to do?*

PONDER: *When I do something that you think God would do if He were here, then you follow that action. Or if I say something kind or wise, remember it, so you can say it to someone else.*

PUPPET 2: *I see. Learning from people who follow God is not like playing "follow the leader."*

PONDER: *No. It's learning to do what God would want you to do wherever you are.*

PUPPET 2: *Oh, I see. I get it. I liked following you though. Let's play "follow the leader." You're it!*

(End.)

RP36: Lily Pads

Cast: Ponder the Frog and Puppet 2

Ponder and Puppet 2 are onstage.

PONDER: *God does know how to help you with any problem.*

PUPPET 2: *Not every problem.*

PONDER: *Yes, He does.*

PUPPET 2: *Okay, if we all breathed really fast at the same time for a long period of time, and we didn't pass out, then we'd use up all the oxygen in the air. How would God solve that?*

PONDER: *He already solved that. He has all the plants breathing out oxygen. New oxygen is made every day.*

PUPPET 2: *Oh. Well, what if all the animals wanted to get from this side of the pond to the other side of the pond without going around it. How would God solve that?*

PONDER: *With a boat. Remember, Noah put all the animals on an ark that God told him to make.*

PUPPET 2: *Oh, yeah. Well, what if I became such a good jumper that I jump so high that I start floating into the sky. How would God solve that?*

PONDER: *Once again, He already has. God made gravity to pull us back down to the earth so that we won't float away.*

PUPPET 2: *Oh. God does seem to solve a lot of problems.*

PONDER: *He's even solved ones that you haven't thought about yet. He knows how to help you.*

PUPPET 2: *Really? He can help me no matter what the problem?*

PONDER: *Of course.*

PUPPET 2: *Whew! That's good news.*

PONDER: *It is.*

PUPPET 2: *Especially for you.*

PONDER: *Me and everyone else.*

PUPPET 2: *Yeah, but right now, you're the one with the problem.*

PONDER: *I don't have any problems.*

PUPPET 2: *You do. I tore your lily pad by accident, and it sunk to the bottom of the pond.*

PONDER: *You what?*

PUPPET 2: *But don't worry. God can solve this.*

PONDER: *Come with me.*

PUPPET 2: *Why? You said God could solve all our problems.*

PONDER: *He can. He's given you to me. You're going to help me pick out a new lily pad.*

(Both exit.)

RP37: Doing What Is Right

Cast: Ponder the Frog and Puppet 2

Ponder and Puppet #2 enter.

PUPPET 2: *Okay. Follow me to the right.*

PONDER: *But the pond is back there.*

PUPPET 2: *Don't worry. I know what I'm doing. You'll thank me in the long run.*

PONDER: *Okay.*

(They move across the stage.)

PUPPET 2: *Let's take a right. (Ponder and Puppet 2 turn their backs to the audience.) And another right. (Ponder and Puppet 2 turn toward the opposite side of the stage. Puppet 2 starts moving toward it.)*

PONDER: *Wait a minute. We're now going in the direction I told you to go in the beginning.*

PUPPET 2: *Of course. I know where the pond is.*

PONDER: *Then why did we go all the way here before going back there?*

PUPPET 2: *Because there is a right and left way to do everything. I am trusting God and doing what is right.*

PONDER: *Right?*

PUPPET 2: *And not left.*

PONDER: *I think you misunderstood the lesson. Doing what is right does not mean you always have to go to your right. It means that you have to do what God wants you to do.*

PUPPET 2: *Are you sure?*

PONDER: *Of course. "Right" can mean a direction, but it can also mean that you are doing what is good before God.*

PUPPET 2: *What a relief. I'm starving, and I couldn't get back to my mother without having to go right around the pond. Thanks, Ponder. This is going to make things a whole lot easier.*

(Exit together.)

RP38: Big Trouble

Cast: Ponder the Frog and Puppet 2

Ponder is onstage. Puppet 2 enters.

PUPPET 2: *Ponder, you're just the frog I was looking for.*

PONDER: *Do you need something,* (Name of Puppet 2)*?*

PUPPET 2: *I do. Do you have any extra food?*

PONDER: *Sure. Are you hungry?*

PUPPET 2: *Oh no. It's not for me. I just had lunch. I want to bring it to some friends who are starving. I've been collecting food for them all morning.*

PONDER: *Did you ask your mother for some?*

PUPPET 2: *Yeah. She gave me a whole bunch. So did all my friends. You're the only one I have left to ask.*

PONDER: *How much food do you need?*

PUPPET 2: *Enough to feed a lot of rabbits—Hopper and Stomper's family.*

PONDER: *I talked with their mother yesterday. She was fine then. What happened?*

PUPPET 2: *Hopper and Stomper's family is so big that their mother asked them each to plant a row of carrots so they'll have plenty of food for the winter.*

PONDER: *That sounds reasonable.*

PUPPET 2: *Hopper and Stomper didn't think so. They organized a club of rabbits who are refusing to work.*

PONDER: *I don't suppose that went over well with their mother.*

PUPPET 2: No. She told them that if they didn't work, they didn't get to eat.

PONDER: So that's why you're gathering food.

PUPPET 2: Yeah.

PONDER: You know, (Name of Puppet 2). **When rabbits disobey their parents, they get in trouble. It's like a nation that disobeys God. When you do something wrong, you suffer the consequences.**

PUPPET 2: You don't think I should bring them food?

PONDER: No. I think their mother knows what is best for them.

PUPPET 2: But if I don't give all this food to Hopper and Stomper's club, what should I do with it?

PONDER: Let's give it to their mother. Just as God knows how to provide for nations, their mother knows how to provide for them. (Looks up at the sun.) If you're going to give her the food, you'd better do it quickly before the vegetables wilt.

PUPPET 2: What vegetables?

PONDER: You did gather food for rabbits, right?

PUPPET 2: Yeah. It's food for them, but I didn't think about what they'd eat. Do rabbits eat tree bark, bananas, and fish?

(Ponder's mouth drops open. End skit.)

RP39: Every Way, Everywhere

Cast: Ponder the Frog, Noah's Park Puppet 2

Ponder is onstage. Puppet 2 enters.

PUPPET 2: *There you are.*

PONDER: *Here I am.*

PUPPET 2: *Stay there. I'll be right back.*

PONDER: *Where are you going?*

PUPPET 2: *To get a marker.*

PONDER: *Why?*

PUPPET 2: *To draw a heart on your back.*

PONDER: *I don't want a heart on my back.*

PUPPET 2: *Of course you do.*

PONDER: *No, I really don't.*

PUPPET 2: *But I have to put one on your back. You're my friend.*

PONDER: *I am your friend, but friends don't let friends draw hearts on their backs with markers. Why would you want to do that anyway?*

PUPPET 2: *I want to love God every day in every way. I am showing it by drawing large hearts on everything and everyone. From all those hearts, God will know how much I love Him.*

PONDER: *That's not what God wants.*

PUPPET 2: *Are you sure? I've just spent the last two hours drawing hearts on everything.*

PONDER: *I'm sure. God wants us to show our love for Him by treating each other well. You just called me your friend. I think that pleased God.*

PUPPET 2:   *Oh. God sees what we do and what we say?*

PONDER: *Exactly.*

PUPPET 2:   *Well, if He can see that, He must have really good eyesight.*

PONDER: *He does.*

PUPPET 2:   *And if He has really good eyesight, then He's going to be able to see all my hearts. So hang on. I've got to go get my marker.*
(Puppet 2 hurries offstage. Ponder groans and shakes his head. End skit.)

RP40: The Emergency

Cast: Ponder the Frog and Noah's Park Puppet 2

Puppet 2 enters with Ponder following.

PONDER: *Can you at least tell me what the emergency is?*

PUPPET 2: *I can't explain it. Look, there it is.*

PONDER: *What?*

PUPPET 2: *The emergency.*

PONDER: *Where?*

PUPPET 2: *There.*

PONDER: *I don't see it.*

PUPPET 2: *Look, there.*

PONDER: *At that tree?*

PUPPET 2: *Yeah. It's been changed. It looks like a giant came by here and twisted its trunk and all of its branches.*

PONDER: *It is gnarled and funny looking, but a twisted tree is not an emergency.*

PUPPET 2: *How can you say that? Whoever twisted that tree had to be enormous. The only person or animal who could have done that would have been a giant. A giant! There's a giant here somewhere! That's an emergency!*

PONDER: *Settle down. A giant didn't do that. Lightning did.*

PUPPET 2: *Lightning? You mean from the storm last night?*

PONDER: *Last night or another one. Sometimes when lightning strikes a tree, it gets twisted like that. I don't know why. It just does.*

PUPPET 2: *But it's so changed.*

PONDER: *Yeah, lightning can change things really fast.*

PUPPET 2: *That's kind of like what God does.*

PONDER: *Only He takes twisted things and makes them right again. But you're right. Believing in Jesus does change people.*

PUPPET 2: *Well, then I guess there is a giant. He just isn't twisting trees.*

PONDER: *I told you, there isn't any—*

PUPPET 2: *If God's big enough to make a storm, then He's a giant in my book. He is so big that He's like a gigantic giant who takes care of us instead of hurting us. He untwists things and changes us when we believe.*

PONDER: *You got it.*

(Exit.)

RP41: Loving God

Cast: Ponder the Frog and Noah's Park Puppet 2

Ponder is onstage. Puppet 2 enters and is shivering.

PUPPET 2: *Ready. Set. Go.* (Prepares to leap.)

PONDER: *Stop!*

PUPPET 2: *Oh, hi, Ponder.*

PONDER: *What are you doing?*

PUPPET 2: *I'm going to stay in the pond for the rest of the day.*

PONDER: *Why? You're shivering. The water's cold.*

PUPPET 2: *I know, but I have to. It's what God wants me to do.*

PONDER: *I don't think God wants you to go back in the pond and catch a cold.*

PUPPET 2: *But He does. You see, my sister's sick. I want to do everything I can to help her get better.*

PONDER: *Jumping into the pond does that?*

PUPPET 2: *Oh yeah. The first day she was sick, I brought her food and water.*

PONDER: *That was nice.*

PUPPET 2: *The second day she was sick, I brought her food, water, and a game to play.*

PONDER: *Good.*

PUPPET 2: *The third day she was sick, I brought her food, water, a game, and stood on my head.*

PONDER: *Why did you stand on your head?*

PUPPET 2: *She said it would help her feel better.*

PONDER: *I see what's happening.*

PUPPET 2: *Then today, when I asked what I could do to help her, she said I could go jump in the pond. So I did. Then I went back to her, and she said I could go jump in the pond and stay there for the rest of the day. I'd better get to it. Ready, set—*

PONDER: *Stop. It's good to do what God wants you to do with a willing heart, like taking care of your sister when she's sick, but He also expects you to use your brain.*

PUPPET 2: *What do you mean?*

PONDER: *I mean that you shouldn't go back into the lake, because your sister is teasing you. Think about it. When your sister was really sick, she needed food and water. Did she ask you for food or water today?*

PUPPET 2: *No.*

PONDER: *As I said, she's teasing you. I'll bet she feels just fine.*

PUPPET 2: *I think you're right. I don't think she's sick at all. If she thinks I'm going to fly to the moon after spending the day in this pond, she has another thought coming.*

(Exit.)

RP42: Giving It Away

Cast: Ponder the Frog and Noah's Park Puppet 2

Ponder and Puppet #2 are onstage.

PUPPET 2: *So you see, I'll give you one blade of grass if you give me your sunglasses.*

PONDER: *I like my sunglasses.*

PUPPET 2: *I'll give you something even better. What if I traded you a cloud for your sunglasses?*

PONDER: *My sunglasses for a cloud? Well, now. That's an offer I can't refuse.*

PUPPET 2: *Really?*

PONDER: *Yeah. Go ahead and get my sunglasses. They're by my lily pad.*

PUPPET 2: *Thanks, Ponder.*

PONDER: *How do I get my cloud?*

PUPPET 2: *Pick any one you want. If you can catch it, you can keep it.* (Puppet 2 laughs and exits.)

PONDER: *(To kids.)* **Don't worry.** (Name of Puppet 2) **didn't trick me. I know that animals can't own clouds. People can't either. I also know that** (Name of Puppet 2) **really wanted my sunglasses. Sometimes when we give to others, it's because we love God.**

PUPPET 2: *(Dejected.)* **I put your sunglasses back. I couldn't go through with the deal. I'm sorry, Ponder. I tried to trick you.**

PONDER: *You did try, but you didn't trick me.*

PUPPET 2: *But you said I could have your sunglasses.*

PONDER: *Yes, I did.*

PUPPET 2: *You mean you knew you would get nothing from me, and you let me have your sunglasses anyway?*

PONDER: *That's what I mean.*

PUPPET 2: *Can I still have them, and give you nothing?*

PONDER: *You can.*

PUPPET 2: *Thanks, Ponder, you're the greatest.* (Puppet 2 hurries off.)

PONDER: *You're welcome,* (Name of Puppet 2). *I'm glad I could help you.*

(Exit)

RP43: True Power

Cast: Ponder the Frog and Noah's Park Puppet 2

Ponder and Puppet 2 are onstage.

PUPPET 2: *I'm sorry, Ponder, but I can't trust you anymore.*

PONDER: *Whether you trust me or not, Jesus' power is still for real.*

PUPPET 2: *Maybe it is. Maybe it isn't. Now there's no way for me to know.*

PONDER: *What have I done that has made you lose your trust in me?*

PUPPET 2: *Oh, you know.*

PONDER: *No, I don't.*

PUPPET 2: *Are you going to make me say it?*

PONDER: *Yeah.*

PUPPET 2: *You lied to me.*

PONDER: *When?*

PUPPET 2: *You told me that rainbows are real, and they aren't.*

PONDER: *Of course they are.*

PUPPET 2: *Fool me once, shame on you. Fool me twice, shame on me.*

PONDER: *Stop with the clichés. Rainbows are real. They are God's promise that He will never flood the earth with water again.*

PUPPET 2: *But they're not real.*

PONDER: *Why do you keep saying that?*

PUPPET 2: *I chased after a rainbow all morning. Whenever I got close to it, it moved away. When I got real close, it disappeared. It's not real.*

PONDER: *I see the problem. By real, you mean that you can touch it.*

PUPPET 2: *Of course.*

PONDER: *God's power is real, but you can't touch it. You can only see the results of it in the world around you. A rainbow is also real, but you'll never be able to touch it either. It is a prism of light caught in the air. It's real, but it's not solid.*

PUPPET 2: *Wow. God is powerful.*

PONDER: *He is, but how did you come to that conclusion?*

PUPPET 2: *He's able to make something that isn't there be there, and no one can ever touch it. Now that's power. Do you think He's powerful enough to move a tree?*

PONDER: *I know He is.*

PUPPET 2: *Good. Because while I was chasing the rainbow, I made an elephant run into a tree, which fell in the place where I usually sleep. I hope God can move it before bedtime.*

(End.)

RP44: Good News/Bad News

Cast: Ponder the Frog and Noah's Park Puppet 2

Ponder and Puppet 2 are onstage.

PUPPET 2: *That's good news.*

PONDER: *No, that was bad news. I had great years as a tadpole, but I always got my way, which made me a little spoiled. I didn't have many friends because of the way I acted.*

PUPPET 2: *That's bad news.*

PONDER: *No, that's good news, because I didn't end up getting into trouble with all of them. I did have one friend, a good friend. She always stood by me . . . after we lost our tails and grew legs, of course.*

PUPPET 2: *That's good news.*

PONDER: *No, that's bad news. I took her friendship for granted. She told me that she thought God wanted us to go on a trip. When I laughed at her, she left without me.*

PUPPET 2: *That's bad news.*

PONDER: *No, that's good news. She did what she felt God was telling her to do even if it meant leaving me behind. I thought about her a lot after she left.*

PUPPET 2: *That's good news.*

PONDER: *No, that's bad news. I realized how selfish I had been. I should have listened to her. I went for days and days in a horrible mood. Nothing made me happy.*

PUPPET 2: *That's bad news.*

PONDER: *No, that's good news. It made me realize that she was my true friend. So, I set off to find her.*

PUPPET 2:   *That's good news.*

PONDER: *No, that's bad news. I couldn't find her anywhere. I did find Noah, though, and he put me into the ark. I was saved. I survived the flood and came to live here.*

PUPPET 2:   *But what happened to your friend? You didn't find her. That's very bad news.*

PONDER: *Actually, it turned out to be good news. You'll never guess who I met on the ark. She was there. She had done just what God told her to do.*

PUPPET 2:   *Now that's good news.*

PONDER: *That was good news. God was with me through all my hard times, and because of Him I'm here today. God is definitely good news.*

(Exit.)

RP45: Saving from Death

Cast: Ponder the Frog, Noah's Park Puppet 2

Ponder is onstage. Puppet 2 hurries onstage.

PUPPET 2: *(Wailing.)* **He's going to die. He's going to die.**

PONDER: *Who is?*

PUPPET 2: **Noah.**

PONDER: *What's wrong with him?*

PUPPET 2: **He's dying.**

PONDER: *Is he sick?*

PUPPET 2: **No.**

PONDER: *What's wrong with him?*

PUPPET 2: **Nothing.**

PONDER: *Then why are you crying and saying that Noah's dying?*

PUPPET 2: **Because he is. Someday he is going to die.**

PONDER: *You had me scared there for a moment.*

PUPPET 2: **You don't care that Noah is going to die someday?**

PONDER: *We're all going to die someday.*

PUPPET 2: *(Wailing.)* **There's no hope. We're all going to die someday. There's no hope at all.**

PONDER: *We are going to die, but there is hope. God promised to send a Savior to break the power that death has over us.*

PUPPET 2: **If He comes soon, does that mean we won't have to die?**

PONDER: *Yes and no. Our bodies are going to die, but what makes us who we are on the inside will live forever. And when people follow the Savior, they get to live with Him in heaven forever.*

PUPPET 2: *That's not so bad.*

PONDER: *Not bad at all.*

PUPPET 2: *How soon can He get here?*

PONDER: *That's up to God. God said that He would send a Savior, so He will.*

PUPPET 2: *I'm sure glad God keeps His promises!*

(All exit.)

RP46: Two in One

Cast: Ponder the Frog, Noah's Park Puppet 2

Ponder and Puppet 2 come onstage together.

PONDER: *I was so hot after the race that I had to get some water.*

PUPPET 2: *Me, too.*

PONDER: *It tasted so good. There's nothing quite like cool water trickling down your throat when you're thirsty.*

PUPPET 2: *You drank it?*

PONDER: *Of course. What did you think I did with it?*

PUPPET 2: *I didn't think you drank it.*

PONDER: *Didn't you just say you drank some water?*

PUPPET 2: *No, I said I had to get some water.*

PONDER: *Doesn't that mean you drank it?*

PUPPET 2: *No, I got some frozen water from my sister. She rubbed ice cubes all over me to help me cool down.*

PONDER: *You weren't thirsty?*

PUPPET 2: *No, but I was really hot. It felt so good.*

PONDER: *That is interesting. We both used water, but I drank it, and you rubbed it over yourself.*

PUPPET 2: *That is weird. Water can take the form of a liquid and a solid.*

PONDER: *Two different forms, but one thing.*

PUPPET 2: *Water is probably the only thing in the world that has two forms like that.*

PONDER: *Well, I'm not so sure about that.*

PUPPET 2: *Are there more?*

PONDER: *I'm sure there are more things in the world with more than one form. But the one I'm thinking of isn't a thing—it's a person. Jesus was all God and all man.*

PUPPET 2: *Jesus was completely God?*

PONDER: *Yep.*

PUPPET 2: *And completely human?*

PONDER: *Yep.*

PUPPET 2: *Wow. Two identities, but one person.*

PONDER: *Yep. Both God and human.*

PUPPET 2: *The only other living thing I know of that has two amazing opposite qualities like that is me.*

PONDER: *You?*

PUPPET 2: *Yeah. I'm handsome, but humble.*

PONDER: *Oh brother. Where's the ice? You need to be cooled down again.*

(Both exit.)

RP47: He's Born!

Cast: Ponder the Frog and Noah's Park Puppet 2

Ponder is asleep onstage. Puppet 2 hurries onstage.

PUPPET 2: *Ponder, wake up!*

PONDER: *(Wakes up.)* **What? Who? What time is it?**

PUPPET 2: **It's the middle of the night.**

PONDER: **Did something bad happen?**

PUPPET 2: **Not that I know of.**

PONDER: *(Lies down.)* **Then I'm going back to sleep.**

PUPPET 2: **No. You can't do that. Get up!**

PONDER: *(Sits up.)* **Is it an emergency?**

PUPPET 2: **No.**

PONDER: **Then good night.** *(Lies down.)* **I'll see you in the morning.**

PUPPET 2: **Ponder! I'm not leaving until you wake up.**

PONDER: *(Sits up.)* **It's the middle of the night. I'm tired. I want to sleep. Can't this wait until morning?**

PUPPET 2: **No, it can't. I need you to come with me.**

PONDER: **And you won't leave me alone until I do?**

PUPPET 2: **That's right.**

PONDER: **Very well. Where are we going?**

PUPPET 2: **To see my new baby sister.**

PONDER: **What? Your mother had a baby? Congratulations,** *(Name of Puppet 2)*.

PUPPET 2: **Isn't it great?**

PONDER: *Yes, it is. I'm glad you woke me up. Your excitement kind of reminds me of how the angels must have felt when Jesus was born.*

PUPPET 2: *Did they say, "Wake up! Jesus is born!"?*

PONDER: *Not in so many words, but that's what they meant. They told shepherds the good news of Jesus' birth, just like you told me.*

PUPPET 2: *It IS good news.*

PONDER: *Let's go and see your new sister.*

(Both exit.)

RP48: Tell Him He's Great

Cast: Ponder the Frog and Noah's Park Puppet 2

Puppet 2 is onstage. Ponder enters.

PONDER: Hi, *(Name of Puppet 2)*. **Why aren't you at** *(Name of Leader's)* **birthday party?**

PUPPET 2: **Why aren't YOU?**

PONDER: **I overslept, but I'm on my way there now. Do you want to hop with me?**

PUPPET 2: **No, I'm not going.**

PONDER: **Why not?**

PUPPET 2: **I don't have a present. I mean I did have a present, but now I don't.**

PONDER: **What happened to your present?**

PUPPET 2: **It was a backscratcher. It took me all week to make, but** *(Name of Leader)* **won't like it.**

PONDER: **Of course she will. She would like anything you give her.**

PUPPET 2: **Even if I accidentally made it out of poison ivy?**

PONDER: **Oh. I see your point.**

PUPPET 2: **Have fun at the party.**

PONDER: **Wait. Do you mean that the only reason you're not going is because you don't have a present for** *(Name of Leader)***?**

PUPPET 2: **Yeah.**

PONDER: **That's no reason.** *(Name of Leader)* **would rather you came and not give her anything.**

PUPPET 2: **But I want to give her something.**

PONDER: *I know. You could tell her something you like about her.*

PUPPET 2: *You mean give her a compliment?*

PONDER: *Yeah. People and animals never hear enough good things about themselves. You could tell her one great memory you have of her, and then thank her for being who God made her to be.*

PUPPET 2: *Is that enough?*

PONDER: *What did the angels bring to Jesus the day He was born?*

PUPPET 2: *The gift of worship.*

PONDER: *What did the shepherds bring to Him?*

PUPPET 2: *Their respect.*

PONDER: *I'm not saying that you should worship* (Name of Leader), *but sometimes being at someone's birth or birthday to show you're glad they're there is enough. Want to go with me to the party?*

PUPPET 2: *I would. If you want, I'll scratch your back as we go.*

PONDER: *No! Let's just walk together.*

(Both exit.)

RP49: Eternal Life

Cast: Ponder the Frog and Noah's Park Puppet 2

Ponder is onstage. Puppet 2 enters in a hurry and runs past Ponder.

PUPPET 2: *Hi, Ponder. Bye, Ponder.*

PONDER: *Where are you going in such a hurry?*

PUPPET 2: *I can't tell you.*

PONDER: *Why not?*

PUPPET 2: *I told Croc I wouldn't.*

PONDER: *Croc? You mean that old, mean crocodile from the next pond over?*

PUPPET 2: *Oops! (Puppet 2 stops.) I wasn't supposed to say his name. Don't tell him I told you.*

PONDER: *What does that rascal Croc want with you?*

PUPPET 2: *I can't tell you about the trip we're going on.*

PONDER: *What trip?*

PUPPET 2: *Oh no. I did it again, didn't I?*

PONDER: *Do your parents know you're going on a trip with Croc?*

PUPPET 2: *No, but they'd be okay with it if they knew I was going to the fountain.*

PONDER: *What fountain?*

PUPPET 2: *Yikes! Me and my big mouth! I promised Croc that I wouldn't tell anyone about going with him to the fountain of youth.*

PONDER: *The fountain of youth? There's no such thing.*

PUPPET 2: *But there is. Croc is going to take me there.*

PONDER: *Think about what you're doing. Croc wants you to do something that you can't tell your parents. Do you think that's smart?*

PUPPET 2: *Not normally—*

PONDER: *And he's taking you far away from your family and friends.*

PUPPET 2: *But that's just because—*

PONDER: *And he's leading you to a mythical place that doesn't exist. The fountain of youth will not give you eternal life, because it isn't real. Only Jesus offers eternal life.*

PUPPET 2: *Oh. When you put it like that, it does sound bad.*

PONDER: *Croc is not your friend. He wants to eat you.*

PUPPET 2: *I'm glad I talked to you before going. That was a narrow escape. Say, do you think there's a city in the clouds?*

PONDER: *No. Why?*

PUPPET 2: *Croc said he'd take me there next week. I suppose this means that that trip is off too.*

PONDER: *It's off. Go tell your parents. And don't forget that only Jesus can give you eternal life and a place in heaven.*

(Puppet 2 hurries off.)

RP50: New Animal

Cast: Ponder the Frog and Noah's Park Puppet 2

Ponder and Puppet 2 are onstage.

PUPPET 2: *Ponder, what am I going to do? That new animal at the pond hates me.*

PONDER: *I'm sure he doesn't hate you.*

PUPPET 2: *Yes, he does. He hates me so much that he told his parents, and now they won't let him play with me.*

PONDER: *I think you might be exaggerating.*

PUPPET 2: *I'm not. The first day I saw him, I went up to him to say hi, but some prankster behind me threw mud at him. He thought I threw it.*

PONDER: *He got mud in his eyes?*

PUPPET 2: *Yeah, and now I can't tell him it wasn't me because his parents keep him far away from me.*

PONDER: *They're just trying to protect him. People and animals usually don't go out of their way to be nice to someone who has been mean to them.*

PUPPET 2: *I guess only God does that.*

PONDER: *You're right. While people were still being mean to God, God sent His Son to die for their sins.*

PUPPET 2: *So what should I do?*

PONDER: *Here, I'll go with you. Maybe I can talk to his parents.*

PUPPET 2: *Should I bring anything?*

PONDER: *No. And maybe you'd better clean your hands before we go. You don't want any mud on them.*

PUPPET 2: *Good idea. I'll be right back.*

PONDER: *And if you have any mud balls in your pockets, take them out.*

(Puppet 2 exits with Ponder following behind.)

RP51: Word Games

Cast: Ponder the Frog, Noah's Park Puppet 2

Ponder and Puppet are onstage.

PUPPET 2: *The word was "crucified."*

PONDER: *What did you say it meant?*

PUPPET 2: *Well, the point of the game was to fool everyone. So I said it described how a snake jumped.*

PONDER: *Snakes don't jump.*

PUPPET 2: *I know. I was trying to be funny. No one guessed my word.*

PONDER: *What definition of the word "crucified" did you guess?*

PUPPET 2: *The wrong one. I guessed that it meant the way Noah drank raspberry juice from a cup.*

PONDER: *Do you know what it really means?*

PUPPET 2: *No. I forgot to listen.*

PONDER: *Let me give you a hint. Jesus was crucified.*

PUPPET 2: *It means that he was nailed to a cross and left to die?*

PONDER: *Yes.*

PUPPET 2: *I don't like that word.*

PONDER: *It is a hard one, but it was a harder thing that Jesus did. That would be because of the word "love."*

PUPPET 2: *I know what that means. It means like when you give your mom a kiss goodnight.*

PONDER: *I have no doubt that you do love your parents, but love means a lot more than a kiss.*

PUPPET 2: *When you kiss both of your parents goodnight?*

PONDER: *It means caring enough for someone that you would be willing to give up your life for them.*

PUPPET 2: *I'm glad that word wasn't in the word game I was playing.*

PONDER: *Why?*

PUPPET 2: *I would never have gotten the right answer.*

RP52: Alive

Cast: Ponder the Frog and Noah's Park Puppet 2

Puppet 2 is talking to the kids. Ponder is watching.

PUPPET 2: **Breathe in.** *(Breathes in deeply.)* **Now breathe out.** *(Breathes out.)* **Kids, do this with me. Breathe in.** *(Breathes in.)* **Breathe out.** *(Breathes out.)*

PONDER: **Why are you breathing like that?**

PUPPET 2: **Because I'm alive.**

PONDER: **I know that when people and animals breathe, they are alive, but why are you breathing like that?**

PUPPET 2: **Because mean people killed Jesus, and He was dead, completely dead. That means that He wasn't breathing. Hey, kids, let's see who can hold their breath with me. Ready, set, go.** *(Puppet 2 holds his breath for a few seconds while Ponder looks between him and the kids. Puppet 2 lets out a breath of air.)* **Wow. You kids are really good at holding your breath. That's as long as I can hold mine.**

PONDER: **I don't get the connection.**

PUPPET 2: **Sorry, I was sidetracked. Where was I?**

PONDER: **You said that mean people killed Jesus, and He was dead.**

PUPPET 2: **That's right. When someone dies, they don't breathe. Jesus died, and He didn't breathe for a lot longer than anyone can hold their breath.**

PONDER: **He didn't breathe for three days.**

PUPPET 2: *Then after three days, He started breathing again, because God raised Him from the dead. He was alive.*

PONDER: *I agree with everything you've said, but I still don't see what that has to do with your deep breathing.*

PUPPET 2: *I've decided to celebrate Jesus' resurrection. Every breath I take helps me remember that Jesus is alive.*

PONDER: *I see. When you breathe in, it's like you're saying, "Thank You, God, for letting me be alive."*

PUPPET 2: *Yeah. And when I breathe out, I think the same thing.*

PONDER: *That's great, (Name of Puppet 2). Let's breathe together.*

PUPPET 2: *Okay. Breathe in. (Ponder and Puppet 2 breathe in deeply.) Now breathe out. (Both breathe out.) Kids, do this with us. Breathe in. (Both breathe in deeply.) Breathe out. (Both breathe out.)*

PONDER: *We're alive, and Jesus is too!*

(End.)

RP53: The Opening

Cast: Ponder the Frog and Noah's Park Puppet 2

Ponder and Puppet 2 walk onstage talking.

PUPPET 2: *And then what happened?*

PONDER: *I hopped across the lily pads to the other side.*

PUPPET 2: *That was great. I didn't know that being a frog could be so exciting.*

PONDER: *It's not all that exciting. It's regular life.*

PUPPET 2: *It sounds exciting to me. I don't know anything about the life of a frog. You just opened a whole new world to me.*

PONDER: *Well, I've told you what I did this morning. Now, you can tell me what you did.*

PUPPET 2: *I didn't do anything.*

PONDER: *Nothing?*

PUPPET 2: *Nothing exciting. I hung around my dad and ripped bark.*

PONDER: *What do you mean you ripped bark?*

PUPPET 2: *It's a game we play.*

PONDER: *I've never heard of it before.*

PUPPET 2: *There's a bunch of hardwood trees on the other side of the pond.*

PONDER: *I know the bunch.*

PUPPET 2: *Well, my dad rips the bark down a line. Then I can rip some off. The best bugs are under that bark.*

PONDER: *I'd like to see that. Let's go over there now.*

PUPPET 2: *It wouldn't do us any good if my dad isn't there. My dad opens the tree for me. Without him, I can't get through the bark to the bugs.*

PONDER: *Interesting. Your dad opens the tree for you just like Jesus opens the Scriptures for us.*

PUPPET 2: *I never thought about it like that. Without Jesus, it would be impossible to understand the Scriptures. Without my dad, it's impossible to eat bark bugs.*

PONDER: *Are the bugs that different?*

PUPPET 2: *No, it's just fun ripping off that hard tree bark to get to them.*

(Both exit.)